The USS Missouri *(BB-63) lies anchored in Tokyo Bay on the morning of 2 September 1945. She is waiting to receive the Japanese delegation that will sign the "Instrument of Surrender" formally ending the Second World War. Mount Fuji, behind the* Missouri*'s for-* *ward 16-inch turret, forms a majestic backdrop for the event. A Baltimore-class cruiser lies beyond the battleship's bow.*

USS MISSOURI (BB-63)

By Robert F. Sumrall

INTRODUCTION

The USS *Missouri* (BB-63) was the third of the four *Iowa*-class battleships to be completed. The *Iowa*s were the most powerful battleships built by the United States, and many feel that they are the most handsome vessels ever designed. Except for four battleships, which are preserved as memorials in the United States, the *Missouri* and her sisters, the *Iowa* (BB-61), *New Jersey* (BB- 62), and *Wisconsin* (BB-64) are the sole survivors of a great fleet of battleships built by all of the major naval powers around the world.

Ships Named Missouri

The USS *Missouri* (BB-63) is the fourth ship in the U.S. Navy to bear the name. It honors the state of Missouri, which was admitted to the Union in 1821 as the twenty-fourth state.

The first *Missouri* was a side-wheel frigate built by the New York Navy Yard and launched 7 January 1841. She was 229 feet long, 40 feet wide, had a mean draft of 19 feet, and displaced 3,220 tons. Her battery was two 10-inch S.B. and eight 8-inch S.B. The *Missouri* was the sixth steam powered vessel in the

U.S. Navy. She was bark-rigged with 19,000 sq. ft. of canvas in plain sails to the top-gallant course. Her steam propulsion was actually considered auxiliary power to assist the sails. While en route to Egypt in 1843, her career was cut short when a storeroom fire spread out of control, and the ship burned and sank off Gibraltar.

The second *Missouri* was a Confederate ironclad, stern paddle-wheel steamer built at Shreveport and launched 14 April 1863. She was 183 feet long, 53 feet 8 inches wide, with a draft of 8 feet 6 inches, and displaced 399 tons. Her battery was one 11-inch S.B., one 9-inch S.B., and one 32 pounder. At the end of the War Between the States, she was surrendered to federal forces 3 June 1865. The CSS *Missouri* was not commissioned in the U.S. Navy. She was dismantled for her iron armor and finally sold at public auction 29 November 1965.

The third *Missouri* (BB-11), one of our early battleships, was built by Newport News Shipbuilding and Dry Dock Co. and was launched 28 December 1901. She was 393 feet 11 inches long, 72 feet 2 inches wide, had a draft of 25 feet 8 inches, and displaced 12,846 tons. Her armament was four 12-inch/40 caliber guns in two twin turrets, sixteen 6-inch/50 caliber guns, six 3-inch/50 caliber guns, and eight 3-pounder guns. Commissioned 1 December 1903, she served with the Atlantic Fleet and in 1907, with fifteen other battleships, took part in the nearly two year around-the-world cruise of Teddy Roosevelt's "Great White

The first Missouri *was a side-wheel steam frigate as shown in this artist's painting. The* Missouri *was one of the very early steam-powered vessels in the U.S. Navy, and her steam propulsion was actually considered auxiliary power for her sails. Launched in 1841, her short career ended on 20 August 1843 when a storeroom fire spread out of control, and she burned and sank off Gibraltar.*

Launched in 1901, the third Missouri *(BB-11) was one of our early battleships. In 1907, she participated in the cruise around the world of the "Great White Fleet." She is shown here about the time of World War I. The* Missouri *was scrapped in 1922 to comply with the Washington Treaty limiting naval armaments.*

Fleet." She served as a training ship for midshipmen and ended her career training recruits during World War I. Decommissioned on 8 September 1919 at Philadelphia, she was finally sold for scrap 26 January 1922 in compliance with the Washington Treaty to limit naval armaments.

THE FAST BATTLESHIP

The concept of the fast battleship resulted from the desire to combine the best features of the battleship and battle cruiser. By general definition, both types carried the same heavy main battery but differed in speed and protection. In theory, battleships were protected against weapons comparable to their own main battery guns by heavy armor plate. On the other hand, battle cruisers were considerably faster but protected by much lighter armor plate. The battle cruiser's speed was intended to compensate, at least in part, for its lighter armor, reasoning that a faster moving target would be harder to track and hit. With the rapid improvement in naval gun fire control, the speed advantage of the battle cruiser steadily declined against the battleship as an opponent. As the new design developed, it was obvious that a fast battleship would have to be considerably larger and heavier than either of the existing types.

To understand the reason for the development of the fast battleship in the U.S. Navy, some background in American naval strategy is helpful. Early in the 20th Century, the United States began to emerge as a significant world naval power. After a successful war with Spain in 1898, the United States was ceded a number of islands in the Pacific and Atlantic oceans and the Caribbean Sea. With this "flash of empire" also came responsibilities. Territorial governments and lines of communication had to be established and maintained, which meant the new areas had to be cared for and protected. A strong navy was essential.

Battleship development in the U.S. Navy had kept pace with all of the major naval powers. Battle cruisers, however, were only in the design stage by the time the United States entered World War I, and the United States was the only major naval power that did not have them during that conflict. Battle cruisers were considered necessary for scouting and raiding and to counter the tactical situation presented by the countries possessing them.

By the end of World War I, the U.S. Navy was in the midst of a huge expansion program. Six 43,200-ton battleships mounting twelve 16-inch guns and six 43,500-ton battle cruisers carrying eight 16-inch guns were under construction. The battleships were to be capable of 23 knots, or only a knot or two faster than the ships in the existing battle fleet, but the battle cruisers were to have a top speed of 33.25 knots and clearly were intended to be among the fastest ships afloat

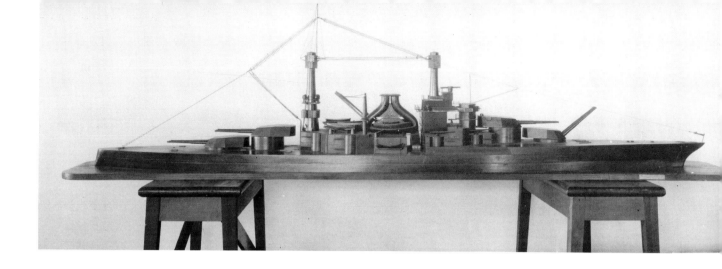

This drawing room model shows the South Dakota *(BB-49) class as they would have appeared. They were to mount 12, 16-inch guns for a main battery and were to be capable of 23 knots. None were completed, and all were scrapped in accordance with the Washington Treaty.*

The Washington Treaty

At the end of World War I, the German High Seas Fleet was dismantled. In 1921, the remaining major naval powers were still attempting to continue their massive building programs. All of the powers engaged in the "Great War" were facing the problems of post-war recession, and could not continue the financial outlay for naval construction much longer.

In the United States, there was little hope that Congress would continue to fund the ambitious building program underway after a costly "war to end all wars." The practical solution was negotiation, the outcome of which was the Washington Treaty of 1922.

The Washington Treaty, which was signed on 6 February 1922, by Great Britain, the United States, Japan, France, and Italy, effected a "building holiday" for ten years. It also restricted the total tonnage that each country could build and further specified the maximum weight and gun caliber of each type of combatant that could be built.

The total tonnage limitations imposed were:
Great Britain - 580,450
United States - 500,320
Japan - 301,320
France - 221,170
Italy - 182,000

This establishment was referred to as the 5-5-3 ratio. Capital ships could not exceed 35,000 tons with a maximum gun caliber of 16-inches. The age of a capital ship was determined to be 20 years, and no new replacement was permitted before that time.

This artist's rendering of the Lexington *(CC-1) shows her final design configuration as a battle-cruiser. The ships of this class were to carry 8, 16-inch guns and have a speed of 33.25 knots. These would have been the first fast capital ships in the U.S. Navy. The* Lexington *and her sister, the* Saratoga *(CC-2), were completed as aircraft carriers, and the rest of the class was scrapped to comply with the Washington Treaty.*

The Japanese battlecruiser Haruma, *shown here at speed in 1934, and her sisters* Kirishima *and* Kongo, *could make 26 knots. This speed advantage over the 21-knot battle line of the American navy drove the design of all future U.S. capital ships.*

Some new vessels could be completed, if they met the treaty restrictions, but most new construction had to be scrapped in order to comply. Many older vessels had to be disposed of to reach the adjusted allotments.

Both the battleship and battle cruiser programs fell victim to the treaty, except for the battle cruisers *Lexington* (CC-1) and *Saratoga* (CC-3), which were completed as aircraft carriers and redesignated CV-2 and CV-3 respectively. As a result of the curtailment of the building program, the U.S. Navy had no capital ships with a high speed capability. The maximum speed of the battle fleet was 21 knots. This was not inconsistent with naval doctrine at that time, because the navy advocated firepower and armor over speed. The problem was, as we shall see, that the treaty allowed potential adversaries to retain capital ships with high speed capabilities.

The conference leading to the treaty produced considerable dissatisfaction and mistrust among the signatory powers. The most bitter disagreement was over the question of total strength allocation. Japan was never satisfied with the 5-5-3 ratio, and feeling forced into a position of inferiority, she eventually withdrew from participation in the 1936 treaty negotiations.

The Probable Enemy

The development of trade with countries in the Far East offered countless commercial opportunities, and after World War I, our national interest gradually shifted to the Pacific. The U.S. Navy began to station major portions of the fleet on the West Coast, and strategic planning was directed toward protecting our possessions and commercial interests in that vast area.

Naval planners assumed that our next war would be with Japan for the domination of the Pacific and that the navy would play a decisive role in the struggle. According to the 5-5-3 ratio, the United States was allowed 15 capital ships and Japan only 9. Of the many battle problems played at the Naval War College, participants always expected that the Japanese would try to reduce this advantage by attrition before any confrontation of battle lines.

In their planning, naval strategists assumed that the Japanese would attack our possessions and commercial shipping. In the event of such an attack, our forces would steam west to protect American interests. They would be at a disadvantage for they would have to pass through a chain of Japanese held islands

The German battlecruiser Scharnhorst *is shown after her July to August 1939 overhaul during which she acquired her "Atlantic bow." Armed with nine 11-inch guns, she and her sister ship* Gneisenau *were capable of making 31.5 knots. They were built in response to the French* Dunkerque *class.*

The French battlecruiser Dunkerque, *launched in 1932, is shown here at anchor during the naval review at Spithead in 1937. The* Dunkerque *and her sister* Strasbourg *were built to counter the three German "Pocket battleships" of the* Lutzow *(ex-Deutschland) class, the first of which was laid down in 1928. The* Dunkerque*s were designed to do 29.5 knots, and during their trials were credited with 31.5 knots.*

on which had been established numerous air and naval bases from which submarines and light, fast ships, such as aircraft carriers and heavy cruisers, could attack our advance units and long lines of communications. The American ships would be struck again as they came within range of land-based aircraft. When the American advantage was sufficiently reduced, the Japanese could then commit their battle line to a decisive engagement.

Three of the Japanese capital ships were the 26-knot *Kongo*-class battle cruisers *Haruna*, *Kirishima*, and *Kongo*. If any of these units were detached from their battle line to assist their carriers and cruisers, they would certainly overpower our carriers and cruisers sent out to counter the enemy. Our 21-knot battle fleet could not bring such fast Japanese task groups to action.

This excellent view shows the 11-inch guns of the German battlecruiser Gneisenau, *taken in 1939 with her sister, the* Scharnhorst *in the background. The German navy was limited to a maximum gun size of 11-inches by the Treaty of Versailles, which formally ended World War I, but was not bound by any other agreement. The class was designed so that the triple 11-inch turrets could be replaced with twin 15-inch turrets. Work actually began on regunning the* Gneisenau *concurrent with the repair of damage received during the "Channel Dash" in February, but was never completed.*

The North Carolina *(BB-55), shown here during her shakedown in 1941, was the first of the U.S. Navy's post-World War I battleships. She mounted nine 16-inch guns, had a displacement limited by treaty to 35,000 tons, and had a maximum speed of 26 knots. Originally designed to carry twelve 14-inch guns, her armor protected her only against that weapon. She was vulnerable to 16-inch gunfire.*

The London Treaties

By the late 1920s, the economic situation throughout the world was not conducive to the beginning of another naval arms race. Yet, in an increasingly paradoxical situation, those countries not at par with Great Britain and the United States wanted equality, even if they couldn't afford it. They saw the possession of giant and powerful floating fortresses as symbolic of their nations' prestige, strength, industrial capability, and scientific achievement.

The Washington Treaty had provided for a conference to be held in London in 1930, a year before the expiration of the building holiday. In an attempt to assume control of naval arms limitations, the League of Nations called instead for a conference to be held in Geneva in 1927. With the Japanese, French, and Italians nursing an accumulation of pent-up grievances from the original conference at Washington, the meeting at Geneva was doomed to failure.

Subsequently, when the second arms limitations conference was convened in London in 1930, the same discontent that had ruined the attempt at Geneva shadowed the talks. By 1930, economic depression had spread throughout the world, and most of the signatory nations could not afford capital ship construction at the cost of their nation's economic survival. The state of the world economy was probably the strongest factor for bringing about eventual agreement at London, and the building holiday was extended for another five years.

The agreement was not without a price. France refused to ratify, justifying her act by the fact that Germany had laid down the "pocket battleship" *Deutschland*, a threat that made new ships necessary as a countermeasure. As expected, Italy also refused to support the treaty, claiming that new French ships would threaten her position in the Mediterranean.

By the time the next naval arms limitations conference was held in London in 1936, a new naval armaments race was well underway. France was building the *Dunkerque* class in answer to Germany's pocket battleships. Italy

countered with a 35,000-ton battleship, which turned out to be over 40,000 tons, and Germany responded to France with the *Scharnhorst* class. The Japanese, meanwhile, announced that they would no longer participate in any agreement to limit naval arms, claiming the right to build as they considered necessary for their national security.

Against this gloomy outlook, the remaining signatory countries inserted an "escalator clause" that would allow them parity with those powers not participating in the treaty. They were required, however, to consult the other signatories before undertaking such a step. Actually this was only a formality to justify the increase in weight and gun size for new construction.

DESIGN BACKGROUND

Design work on the navy's new battleships was begun in 1935, and there was no question that an increase in speed was of primary concern. In July of 1935, the General Board[1] asked the Bureau of Construction and Repair (BuC&R) for design sketches of a 35,000-ton battleship capable of steaming at 30 knots and armed with either 14- or 16-inch guns.[2] A design was prepared with nine 14-inch guns in triple turrets, capable of 30 knots, and within the 35,000-ton weight limitation. After some consideration, the Board rejected the design because the main battery was considered inadequate. The BuC&R reworked the design, coming up with a ship that mounted twelve 14-inch guns in three quadruple turrets. The three additional 14-inch guns had their price. To stay within the 35,000-ton treaty limit, a three-knot reduction in speed had to be accepted. The result was the *North Carolina* class.

The *North Carolina* (BB-55) was laid down on 3 June 1936, and studies for the next generation of battleships, which would become the *South Dakota* class, were immediately begun. When the Japanese withdrew from participation in the 1936 Treaty, they also refused to state that they would not adopt 16-inch

Still limited by treaty to 35,000 tons, the South Dakota *class represented a major improvement over the* North Carolinas*. With a main battery of nine 16-inch, guns, they were somewhat shorter than their predecessors. The weight saved because of the* South Dakota*'s shorter hull was allocated to additional protection and machinery, which gave her immunity to 16-inch gunfire and a speed of 27 knots. In this photo, taken 4 June 1942, the* South Dakota *(BB-57) is leaving Philadelphia en route to the Pacific.*

guns in their new designs. As a result, by mid-1937, the U.S. Navy had decided to adapt the 16-inch gun in all new construction.[3] The General Board asked the Bureau of Ordnance (BuOrd) to design a new triple 16-inch turret for the *North Carolina* class. Nine 16-inch guns would replace the twelve 14-inch guns in the new battleships. The next generation of designs then in progress would also receive the new guns. The U.S. Navy's decision to increase the gun caliber to 16-inch on all new battleships would prove to be a wise one.

A battleship is designed to resist gunfire comparable to its own main battery. In theory, it would overpower a weaker adversary and avoid contact with a more powerful one. When the General Board made the decision to increase the size of the main battery in *North Carolina*, she was already too far along in construction to increase her armor protection. Any increase in armor also would have put her well over the weight limit, which was unacceptable.

Naval designers felt that the *North Carolina* represented the limit of what could be attained on 35,000 tons, and that in some areas, she was even badly compromised. Yet the new design, which became the *South Dakota* class, was armed with nine 16-inch guns, was protected against them, was capable of 27 knots, and did not exceed the 35,000-ton limit.

A number of adjustments and accommodations to the *North Carolina* design were necessary and, indeed, the key to the success of the new design. First, maximum protection for the least possible weight was achieved by placing the armor belt inboard, inclining it to 19 degrees, extending it downward, and tapering it to 1 inch at its lower edge. Second, a unique and radically new machinery arrangement was devised with boilers above turbines in the same space. This allowed a considerable reduction in length. Finally, all uptakes were trunked into one funnel, and with other topside rearrangements, the superstructure was shortened to be compatible with the spaces below in the hull. These were not easy solutions, because they required a great deal of advanced engineering design and development. Also, the arrangement was somewhat cramped, but the design was

viable, and it proved to be very successful.

Design requirements were finalized in August 1937, and after preparation of contract plans and specifications, the *South Dakota* was laid down on 5 July 1939.

1. The General Board was a group of senior naval officers representing the Office of the Chief of Naval Operations and the Bureaus of Construction and Repair, Engineering, Ordnance, and Navigation. The Board's primary purpose was to determine the mission requirements for each type of vessel and the characteristics necessary to carry out their missions in order to implement national policy.

2. The second London Conference would be convened the following year, and the somewhat ambiguous instructions reflected the Board's uncertainty concerning the maximum gun caliber that would be allowed.

3. Japan guarded her naval construction program with extreme security measures. After three years of design studies, a building plan was approved in March 1937, and the first new battleship that Japan built was laid down at Kure Navy Yard on 4 November 1937. Almost immediately, the shipway was shrouded with huge tarpaulins to prevent observation of design characteristics and building progress. Intelligence reports credited the vessel as over 45,000 tons and with 16-inch main armament. Some reports speculated on an even larger vessel armed with 18-inch guns. The vessel was the *Yamato*, and the latter speculations proved correct.

The keel of the Missouri *is "truly and fairly laid" on 6 January 1941 at the New York Navy Yard. RAdm. C. H. Woodward, Chief of the Bureau of Construction and Repair, drove the first rivet.*

THE IOWA DESIGN

The interest in a fast battleship had by no means diminished, and the Preliminary Design Section of the BuC&R conducted various studies of such a vessel after the completion of the *South Dakota* design.

The U.S. Navy had already wisely adopted the 16-inch gun, and now it appeared that potential adversaries had actually begun construction of battleships well in excess of the 35,000-ton limit. At this point, it certainly appeared that the 1936 treaty signatory powers would raise the total per ship weight to 45,000 tons.

Early in 1938, the General Board asked for a new study of a fast battleship to determine just what 45,000 tons would buy. The study indicated that an expanded *South Dakota* capable of 33 knots was feasible on the new tonnage. This was the beginning of the *Iowa*-class design.

In addition to the 33-knot speed, another feature of the new design was a 16-inch/50 caliber gun. This was to have been the main armament for the battleships and battle cruisers canceled in 1922. Although a number of them were available from inventory, the BuOrd developed a new lightweight 16-inch/50 caliber gun, the MK 7. This weapon was preferred over the 16-inch/45 caliber gun installed in the *North Carolina* and *South Dakota* classes because of its greater range and penetration.

The BuC&R submitted the new characteristics to the General Board on 2 June 1938, at the same time that the agreement to escalate the treaty was being signed. The Board responded with directions for the BuC&R to go ahead with the contract plans and specifications and the BuOrd with the design of the new 16-inch/50 caliber turret.

Design proceeded at an accelerated pace, and by November 1938, the contract plans were complete, and then, the designers discovered a potentially serious discrepancy in specifications for the new gun turret. The turret designed by the BuOrd did not fit in the space allotted by the BuC&R hull design. At this point, the hull could not be altered without changing its efficiency, which meant a reduction in speed. An alternative would have been a reversion to the 16-inch/45-caliber turret, which would easily fit. Neither of these plans was acceptable—an additional 10,000 tons would achieve little or nothing. Directed to redesign the turret, the BuOrd produced a turret with a barbette diameter small enough to meet all of the installation requirements of the BuC&R's design.

Originally, the General Board had envisioned three fast battleships to counter the three Japanese Kongos, and Congress appropriated funds for two ships in Fiscal Year 1940. These became the *Iowa* (BB 61) and *New Jersey* (BB 62). The New York Navy Yard was selected to build the lead ship and prepare the working plans for the class. The Philadelphia Navy Yard was awarded construction of the second ship. On 1 July 1939, with contracts signed, the New York Navy yard formally began the construction and manufacturing drawings.

The design of the *Iowa*s and, in particular, their system of armor protection was predicated on the main battery using the 2,240-pound AP shell then in use. In June 1939, the BuOrd proposed a new 16-inch shell weighing 2,700 pounds to replace the 2,240-pound shell. Although the heavier shell had a lower velocity, it retained its velocity longer, and the new lower muzzle velocity increased the life and accuracy of the gun. The new shell was adopted. The *Iowa* class was designed to resist the 2,240-pound shell and an increase in armor for protection against the heavier shell was quite impossible on 45,000 tons. (See armor protection for the effects on immunity.)

By expanding the *South Dakota* design, the size of the machinery spaces grew considerably to accommodate the increase in horsepower from 130,000 HP to 212,000 HP. In the *South Dakota*, each machinery space was only forty feet long. In the new design, however, the combination engine-room fire-room arrangement created four enormous compartments amidships each sixty-four feet in length. This meant that a single shell penetration at one of the main bulkheads would flood 128 feet. Therefore, the New York Navy Yard proposed an alternating fire room, engine room arrangement with two boilers in each fire room and one set of machinery in each engine room for its propeller shaft. This allowed the four large machinery spaces to be broken up into eight thus reducing the flooding potential from a single hit by half. This also simplified the trunking of the uptakes

These construction progress photographs of the Missouri show many design features that will be obscured when the vessel is completed. Above left: In this view looking aft, all eight boilers are in place, the tunnel stern and twin skegs are taking shape, the torpedo defense system is clearly, visible, and the armor belt, inclined at 19 degrees, is being hung. Above right: This view, taken at the same time but looking forward, shows many of the same features and the fine entrance of the bow. Both views give a clear indication of the minute subdivision of the machinery spaces. Below left: Looking aft from barbette No.1, the ship is nearing the launching stage with work progressing above the 03 level. Splinter protection for the light antiaircraft battery is being installed and, to port, the teak deck is being laid. Below right: Looking forward from the same position shows most of the deck fittings installed. Splinter protection for the light anti-aircraft battery on the bow has been erected, and the wooden deck is being laid.

Minutes after launching, on 29 January 1944, the Missouri comes to a stop in the East River to await the tugs that will take her to a berth in the outfitting basin in the New York Navy Yard. There she will be completed and commissioned for service.

The port propellers, skeg, and rudder are clearly visible in this 23 July 1944 photo taken in dry dock at the New York Navy Yard. Note the 18´ 3″ four-bladed propeller outboard and the 17' 0" five-bladed propeller inboard.

Ready for launching, the massive battleship is truly impressive. As seen here, her extremely fine lines forward can be fully appreciated. This view also shows the full shape of the underwater bulb of the Missouri's distinctive clipper bow. The large external hawse pipe castings were designed to allow the anchor's flukes to clear the bulb as it was raised or lowered. The 20mm gun platform atop the stem is another distinguishing feature of the class.

Nearing completion, the Missouri *is being outfitted at one of the piers in the New York Navy Yard. Completion of the battleship took nearly five months after she was launched. Of particular interest in this photo is the huge hammerhead crane on the pier just behind the bridge. The capacity of the crane was great enough to lift fairly large pieces of super-structure into place on the hull allowing a consider-able amount of prefabrication.*

to the funnels and reduced the size of penetrations through the armored decks. BuC&R approved the new machinery arrangement and contract plans were revised accordingly. From a damage control and survivability point of view, the delays and expenses incurred by making such significant design changes were well worth the benefits gained.

The navy expected to build two more battleships in Fiscal Year 1941, BB-63 and BB-64. BB-63 was to be a fast battleship, but BB-64 was planned as a slower version, possibly with twelve 16-inch guns. The War Plans Division now objected, reasoning that they wanted a clear-cut superiority in numbers of fast battleships. The General Board finally agreed, and on 12 June 1940, the *Missouri*

With her outfitting complete, the Missouri *awaits her final dry docking before being commissioned. Note how the huge hammerhead crane dwarfs the ship. The crane could easily lift the main battery's 16-inch barrels, which weighed nearly 240,000 pounds.*

This topside view shows the Missouri *in dry dock at the New York Navy Yard on 23 July 1944, preparing for her shakedown cruise. Much of the ground tackle forward is visible on the forecastle. Note the anchor chain and "pelican hook" chain stoppers. Each die-lock link measures 22 inches overall. A 15-fathom shot weighs 12,500 pounds. The small "wild-cat" to starboard is for hauling the paravane chain, and the sheave directly forward directs the chain through a pipe to the forefoot fair leader.*

(BB-63) was ordered from New York Navy Yard, and the *Wisconsin* (BB-64) from Philadelphia Navy Yard as fast battleships.

With what it considered a "sufficient number of fast battleships," the General Board ordered studies resumed on the BB-65-class of slower, heavier battleships. Congress authorized a large emergency construction program on 19 July 1940, which included two battleships. The General Board wanted these two units to be of the new design, but BB 65 was not far enough along. The Secretary of the Navy directed that the new ships be duplicates of those already designed and under construction. On 9 September 1940, the *Illinois* (BB-65) was ordered from the Philadelphia Navy Yard, and the *Kentucky* (BB-66) was ordered from the Norfolk Navy Yard as units of the *Iowa* class.

General Arrangement

In general, the primary consideration for the new class of battleships was high speed. Externally, speed meant fine hull lines and extreme length; internally the same fine hull lines meant relatively little volume into which barbettes, ammunition, control stations, fuel, supplies, the crew, and 212,000-shaft horsepower could be fitted. The superstructure also had to be compact, so as not to unduly restrict the arcs of fire of the guns and the visibility of the fire control gear. A great deal of the superstructure proper was filled with gun mounts, ammunition hoists, directors, and director tubes, leaving a limited amount of space available for accommodations.

There were three continuous decks: the main or weather deck, which served as the bomb deck; the second deck, which was the principal armored deck; and the third, which covered the machinery spaces. A splinter deck was fitted directly below the second, or main armored deck, and extended from barbette No. 2 to barbette No. 3. The splinter deck was not a full deck height and was placed so close to the second deck that the space between them was not really usable. Interrupted amidships by the machinery spaces, the lower decks were "platforms" that formed decks forward and aft. From the third deck down were the first, second, and third platform decks. The hold was the next deck below the third platform and extended from forward of barbette No. 1 to aft of barbette No. 3 and the flat that carried the foundations for the main machinery. The hold formed a triple bottom beneath the vitals of the ship on top of the double bottom, which formed a continuous flat from the stem to aft of barbette No. 3.

Below the third deck were eight main machinery spaces with an alternating fire room, engine room arrangement located approximately between the conning tower and the after main battery director.

The magazines for the 16-inch guns were forward and aft of the machinery spaces and rested on the inner bottom. The largest part of the magazines was used for powder stowage. Most of the projectiles were stowed in rings rotating

Above: the Missouri *is anchored off Bayonne, New Jersey, in August 1944, after returning from her shakedown and trials. A barge alongside is taking off refuse from her cruise. Above right: the bridge and main fire control tower display her original radar and electronics equipment. A periscope for the MK 40 director can be seen above the conning tower with its MK 27 radar. Just abaft is a MK 37, 5-inch director with its MK 12/22 radar above. Atop the tower is a MK 38, 16-inch director with its MK 8 radar. The 17-foot dish of the SK-2 air search radar is above and aft of the 16-inch director. Highest up is the SG surface search radar.*

In this view, taken 23 July 1944, the Missouri is in dry dock at the New York Navy Yard making preparations to get underway for her shakedown cruise. The massive anti-aircraft battery amidships is clearly visible. Note the gallery of quadruple 40mm mounts between the stacks, the single 20mm galley just below, and the battery of twin 5-inch mounts on the 01 and 02 levels below. Two 36-inch searchlights are also visible, one each at the forward and after stacks.

In another view taken 23 July 1944, nearly all of the elements of her original fire control and radar suite are visible. The MK 38 main battery directors with their MK 8 radar are atop the fire control towers. Three of the four MK 37 5-inch directors, with their MK 12/22 radars, are on each side of the forward funnel and the after superstructure. The SK-2 air search radar is on the foretop, and the two SG surface search sets are atop the foremast and mainmast. The "skipole" antennas for the BK (IFF) transponders can be seen on both the foreyard and main yard.

A view looking forward from near the stern, also taken on 23 July 1944, shows No. 3 turret of the main battery trained out to port. Floater-net storage has not been completed, and fair weather companions are being fitted to the main access hatches. Many civilian yard workers and their equipment are still aboard, and a dolly for storing the aircraft on the catapults or on deck is at the far left. Note that two visiting ladies have just come aboard over the port gangway.

with and hung from the turret mechanism and on shelves supported from the inner sides of the barbette.

The superstructure rose above the main deck in two continuous levels. All of the ten 5-inch/38 caliber twin gun mounts were concentrated on these two decks designated the 01 and 02 levels. A heavy armored conning tower, from which the ship was commanded in battle, was located near the forward end of the superstructure. The navigating bridge was at the 04 level around the conning tower, and the pilot house was directly aft. Accommodations for the captain and the flag were below the pilot house.

The primary conning station was at the 08 level on the forward fire control tower. The forward main battery director was atop the tower with the center of its stereoscopic rangefinder 116 feet above the waterline.

There were two large funnels, indicative of the ship's massive power plant. The leading edge of the forward funnel was faired into the fire control tower, and the flue gasses were vented from a flat slightly above the primary conning position. The after funnel was free-standing and vented slightly lower than the forward one. Large caps were placed on each funnel to direct the gases aft. The centers of the uptakes were nearly 100 feet apart, and the primary portion of the 40-mm air defense battery was in a cluster between them.

Aft of the second stack was the after fire control tower with a second main battery director atop. The centerline of its range finder was 68 feet above the waterline. Weight and stability would not allow the after director to be as high as the forward one, therefore, it was installed low enough in most cases to avoid the gases from the second funnel.

Above: tugs guide the Missouri *away from the dock at the Bremerton Group, U.S. Pacific Reserve Fleet on 14 May 1984. She was towed to the Long Beach Naval Shipyard to undergo reactivation and modernization that would take about two years. Below: tugs assist the* Missouri *toward the dock at Long Beach Naval Shipyard to begin her reactivation/modernization. Note the "igloos" used to protect the 40mm gun mounts while the ship was in reserve.*

MODERNIZATION

The *Missouri* served continuously from her first commissioning on 11 June 1944 until she fell victim to post-World War II austerity policies. She was decommissioned on 26 February 1955 and placed in the Atlantic Reserve Fleet at Philadelphia.

After World War II, the *Missouri* received the latest radar, electronics, and communications suites, including a heavier main mast to carry the additional weight of the new equipment. Except for these changes, her configuration was nearly identical to that of her wartime service.

During the campaign in Korea, her 16-inch batteries proved invaluable for shore bombardment, supporting the ground forces in the seesaw war underway there. After the Korean truce, the *Missouri* remained active until she was decommissioned in 1955.

During the Vietnam War, the *New Jersey* was activated for a brief time, but none of the other ships of the *Iowa* class were seriously considered for reactivation. As was the case in Korea, the battleship's 16-inch guns provided valuable fire support for the U.S. Marine Corps and Army forces along the coastline.

The four ships of the *Iowa* class remained in the reserve fleet surviving various attempts at disposal. Surveys during the mid- and late-1970s showed them all to be in good material condition with considerable service life remaining. The first serious consideration for reactivation and modernization was in 1980. The *New Jersey* was included in the FY 81 budget, but she did not survive the budget-cutting process. In a second attempt, she was included in the FY 81 supplemental budget and finally won approval. This was the beginning of the new battleship program, which eventually saw all four of the *Iowa*s modernized and recommissioned for service in the "600-Ship Navy" of the 1980s.

The mission of the modernized *Iowa*s was to conduct prompt and sustained combat operations at sea. They were capable of destroying surface, air, and shore targets with both guns and missiles and were capable of being projected into a number of other roles. In a surface-action group, a battleship was the principal ship. Its 16-inch guns were unmatched in power and accuracy, and the Harpoon and Tomahawk cruise missiles gave the battleship a long-range strike capability. The great speed of the *Iowa*s enabled them to combine operations with a carrier battle group to form what could be called a super strike group. They were ideally suited for operating in areas of lesser threat, which enabled the more effective deployment of carriers elsewhere. In providing surface protection, shore bombardment, and gunfire support to amphibious operations, the Iowas brought back the pinpoint accuracy of the big gun, which is sorely lacking in the 1990s.

Surface warfare capabilities were significantly increased. New weapons systems included thirty-two long-range Tomahawk cruise missiles in armored box launchers, sixteen medium-range Harpoon cruise missiles in armored canister launchers, and four Close In Weapons System (CIWS) gatling guns for defense

For the traditional stepping of the mast, the photo above shows the medallion, enclosing a representative coin, placed beneath the mast and the plaque presented to the commanding officer with representative coins of the three commissionings of the USS Missouri (BB-63). Left: The inscription on the medallion reads "Stepping ceremony, Long Beach Naval Shipyard, 9 April 1985, Commemorative coin enclosed." Right, the inscription on the plaque reads "This plaque is presented to Captain A. L. Kaiss, PCO, Missouri on 9 April 1985, by Captain G. E. Fink shipyard commander, representing the employees of the Long Beach Naval Shipyard. The coins below represent the coins used to commemorate the traditional stepping of the mast on this date." The first coin, "Commissioning, USS Missouri (BB-63), June 11, 1944;" the second, "Formal Surrender of Japan to Allied Forces, September 2, 1945;" and third, "New mast installed on USS Missouri (BB-63) during reactivation, April 9, 1985."

The traditional stepping of the mast ceremony on the Missouri at the Long Beach Naval Shipyard on 9 April 1985. Note the giant crane at the right, which is lowering the new lattice tripod mast into position.

Above: the Missouri *is nearing completion of her two-year reactivation and modernization at the Long Beach Naval Shipyard. Some scaffolding is still in place, and the barges and floating crane on her port side are beginning to offload the last of the shipyard equipment and material. Below: All work has been completed in this 8 May 1986 photo and the* Missouri *is making final preparations for getting under way for her recommissioning at San Francisco on 10 May.*

against airborne attack. Sensor capabilities were updated to include the Two Dimensional (2-D), SPS-49 long-range air search radar, the SPS-10 or SPS-67 surface search radar, a cruiser-size communications suite with a Naval Tactical Data System (NTDS) LINK 11 receiver for Tomahawk control and LINK 14 for receipt of tactical data. New Electronic Counter Measures (ECM) equipment consisted of the SLQ-32(V) 3 ECM system, eight MK 137 SRBOCK chaff launchers, and the SLQ NIXIE torpedo defense system. Supporting systems updates included converting the boilers to burn Diesel Fuel Marine (DFM), the installation of a Sewage Collection, and Holding (CHT) system, and the provision for 400 Hz power.

The arguments for keeping the battleships in service were compelling. Their presence as a platform for heavy guns and long range missiles far outweighed the costs associated with their active service. Except for the carriers, they were more expensive to operate than most surface ships, but their capabilities were many times greater. For example, against a typical shore bombardment target, an Iowa's 16-inch guns could deliver conventional munitions, in tons per hour, at a rate of about two and one half times faster than all of the aircraft of a carrier. In addition, both the 16-inch armor-piercing and high-capacity shells had greater penetrating capability against hardened targets than any aircraft-dispensed ordnance. In a routine mission of this type, it would be unnecessary to commit valuable aircraft and their crews to provide fire power against coastal targets.

Another dimension that the battleship brought to surface warfare was survivability. This is not to imply that a battleship could not be sunk, but to sink one would be a difficult task indeed. Their heavy armor, torpedo defense system, and watertight subdivision would not be easily defeated by any conventional weapons, including cruise missiles such as the Exocet. In contrast, an Aegis cruiser has no armor and no protection against torpedoes and mines. Although the torpedo and mine defense systems of a carrier are comparable to those of a battleship, a well placed bomb or cruise missile could seriously disrupt, if not terminate, all flight operations of the super-carriers, leaving them with no strike or defense capabilities.

The battleships, however, were competing for funding in the Navy's budget and critics of the program were quick to point this out, even though, the cost to modernize and recommission a battleship apparently was less than the cost of a new frigate. Nonetheless, the ships were finally decommissioned: the Iowa and New Jersey in 1990 and the Missouri and Wisconsin in 1991.

All reactivation and modernization work completed the Missouri, with her crew "manning the rail" turns into the stream as she leaves the Long Beach Naval Shipyard for San Francisco.

Heading out of Long Beach Naval Shipyard on 8 May 1986, the Missouri turns north and begins her run to San Francisco where she will be commissioned on 10 May.

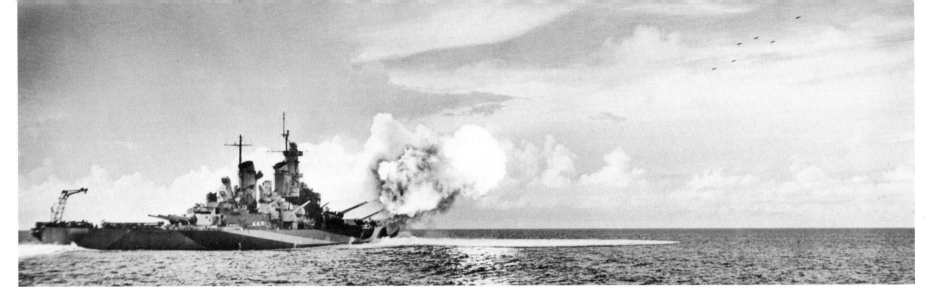

The Missouri *fires a salvo from turrets No. 1 and No. 2 in August 1944 during her shake-down cruise. Note the six projectiles in flight, at the right, which have just left the muzzles of the guns. A six-shell salvo of 2,700-pound armor piercing rounds weighs a total of* 16,200 *pounds. A full nine-shell salvo would weigh a total of 24,300 pounds. The maximum range of the 2,700-pound shell was 40,185 yards, or about twenty-three miles.*

ARMAMENT

Main Battery: 16-inch Guns

The main armament of the Missouri was the 16-inch/50 caliber MK 7 gun.[4] Nine guns were mounted in three 3-gun turrets.[5] The gun was a lightweight, built-up-type consisting of a liner, tube, jacket, hoops, locking rings, a liner locking ring, and a yoke locking ring. Assembly involved heating and expanding each piece before sliding it into position over the tube. When the components cooled and shrank, a tight single unit was formed. The liner was rifled with 96 grooves 0.15 inches deep, with a uniform right hand twist of one turn in 25 calibers. Each gun was mounted on an individual slide with its own elevation drive. The assembly included a breach mechanism, firing lock, gas ejector, and yoke. The individual gun and slide assemblies, the two sight stations, and the rangefinder's station were located in separate, flame proofed compartments in each turret.

The turrets were virtually identical, each consisting of an armored gun house with a rotating structure and a fixed structure. The gun pit and machinery flat extended below the shelf plate of the gun house, and the upper roller track was attached to the underside of the pit pan plate. A central column extended down to the turret foundation supporting the rotating handling, or shell decks. The fixed structure was a circular foundation bulkhead, or stool. The lower roller track was atop the stool, and the rotating structure was supported by roller bearings between the roller tracks. The fixed handling, or shell decks, were supported from the stool sides. Turrets I and III had two shell decks. Turret II, which was a deck higher, had three. The turret structure was protected by a barbette of heavy armor. There was a weather seal between the barbette and the gun house, but the gun house was not supported by, nor did it rotate on the barbette. Most of the projectiles were stored on the fixed (outer) and rotating (inner) shell decks. Powder handling rooms were at the base of each stool adjacent to the magazines.

Each turret could be trained at the rate of 4 degrees per second, and the guns could be elevated at the rate of 12 degrees per second, either together or individually. The guns could be elevated to 45 degrees and depressed 5 degrees. Loading was at a fixed angle of 5 degrees elevation. The guns were capable of firing at the rate of two rounds per minute. The normal allowance was 100 rounds per gun, but magazine space for 120 rounds per gun was provided.

---

4. During the early 1938 studies, which led to the *Iowa* class, the General Board seriously considered using the 18-inch/47 caliber gun developed by the BuOrd during the 1920s. Although it did present some disadvantages, the 16-inch/50 caliber was considered an all around better weapon.

5. They were designated three-gun turrets, as opposed to triple turrets, because each gun was mounted on an individual slide with its own elevation drive. A triple turret had a single slide providing bearing surfaces for all three guns and used a common elevation drive.

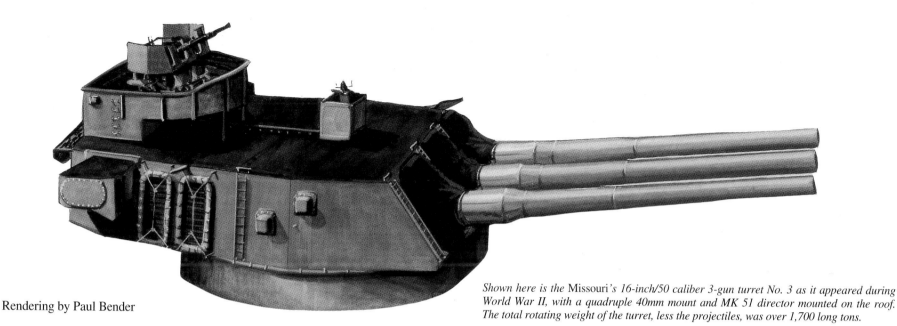

Rendering by Paul Bender

Shown here is the Missouri's *16-inch/50 caliber 3-gun turret No. 3 as it appeared during World War II, with a quadruple 40mm mount and MK 51 director mounted on the roof. The total rotating weight of the turret, less the projectiles, was over 1,700 long tons.*

Main Battery: Projectiles

The MK 7 gun fired two basic rounds: a 2,700-pound armor piercing (AP) and a 1,900-pound high capacity (HC) shore bombardment projectile.

The AP projectile was the MK 8 with a 1.5% bursting charge. It used the MK 21 Base Detonating Fuze/.033 sec. delay (BDF) and required a resistance equal to 1.5 inches of armor for activation. Full, special, and reduced charges were used with the MK 8 projectile. The special and reduced charges, with their resultant lower muzzle velocity, gave the projectile a steeper angle of fall and a trajectory similar to the 16-inch/45 caliber gun (see Ballistic Data). The effect of the steeper trajectory was to shrink an armored surface target's immune zone at the outer end. It also enhanced defilade (reverse slope) capability against land targets.

The standard HC shore bombardment projectile was the MK 13 with a 8.1 percent bursting charge. It used either the MK 29 Point Detonating Fuze (PDF) or the MK 48 BDF. Two special MK 13 HC projectiles used steel nose plugs. The first used a MK 55 Auxiliary Detonating Fuze (ADF) and a MK 48 BDF. The second used a MK 21 BDF. Another MK 13 High Explosive (HE) projectile was fuzed with a M564 Mechanically Timed Fuze/100-second capability (MTF).

Four special-purpose projectiles using the MK 13 body were developed during the 1980s. They were the MK 143 HE, which used the Army M732 Controlled Variable Time (CVT) proximity fuze; the MK 144 Improved Conventional Munitions (ICM) fuzed by the M724 Electronically Timed Fuze (ETF), which dispensed 400 M43A1 wedge grenades; the MK 145 HE with the M724 ETF; and the MK 146 ICM using the M724 ETF, which dispensed 666 shaped charge bomblets.

A sub-caliber extended-range projectile was under development during the 1980s. It was a spin stabilized 13-inch (approx.) body with a sabot adapting it to the 16-inch bore. The sabot was discarded after the projectile left the muzzle. The flight weight of the projectile was 1,000 pounds and when fired with a full charge of powder, it had a muzzle velocity of greater than 3,600 ft./sec. It was capable of ranges in excess of 70,000 yards.

Main Battery: Propellant

Propelling charges for the guns used smokeless powder, or SP, which is a uniform ether-alcohol colloid of purified nitrocellulose. A small quantity of diphenylamine, or ethel centrality, was added for stability. Other additives were used to obtain suitable form, burning character, and stability. After the manufacturing process, a finished grain of 16-inch powder was approximately two inches long and one inch in diameter with seven small perforations running the length of the grain.

The 16-inch guns were termed "bag guns," because the propellant charge was contained in cylindrical bags, which were loaded separately from the projectiles. The guns required a large amount of powder for the projectile to attain its required initial velocity. If the powder was placed in a single container, the size and weight would greatly complicate the powder-handling machinery. By breaking up the charge into sections and packing the powder grains in fabric bags, the

sections could be easily handled by the turret crew.

The powder bag was made of silk so that it would completely burn away when the charge was ignited. The powder was loaded into the bags either by stacking or dumping the grains. In a stacked charge, the grains were arranged in layers with their axes parallel to that of the bag. In an unstacked charge, the grains were randomly dumped into the bag. An ignition pad containing black powder was quilted to the back of each bag to ensure instant ignition between bags. The ignition pad was usually colored red for proper alignment of the charge. A typical bag for a standard charge weighed about 110 pounds.

Two types of 16-inch/50 caliber SP propellants were used. They were coded according to the Naval Ammunition Logistics Code/Department of Defense Inventory Code (NALC/DODIC) as D839 and D846. D839 was the original 16-inch/50 caliber powder and D846 was the 16-inch/45 caliber powder. D839 was used with the MK 8 and MK 13 type projectiles, but D846 was used only with the MK 13 projectile.

Each time a gun was fired, the rotating band of the projectile eroded the liner as it traveled the length of the bore. Gun life was expressed as the number of Equivalent Service Rounds (ESR) that could be fired before the gun had to be relined. As designed, the life of the 16-inch/50 caliber MK 7 gun was determined to be 290 ESR, based on the 2,700 AP projectile fired with a full charge, which produced a muzzle velocity of 2,500 ft/sec. During the 1980s, wear-reducing jackets for the powder bags were developed. Made of titanium dioxide, wax, and polyurethane foam, they greatly reduced liner erosion, in some cases by as much as 60 percent.

Secondary Battery: 5-inch Guns

The secondary battery of the *Missouri* was the double-purpose 5-inch/38 caliber MK 12 gun. As originally designed, the battery consisted of twenty 5-inch guns in ten MK 28 twin gun mounts. Two mounts were on each side of the 01 level and three were on each side of the 02 level. Because the large superstructure restricted their arcs of fire, they were most effective against targets approaching abeam. The crowded superstructure did not allow placing any 5-inch mounts on the centerline. During the 1985–1986 modernization, the battery was reduced by eight guns. The aftermost mounts on each side of the 02 level were removed to make room for the addition of missile batteries. The turrets could be rapidly trained, the guns elevated to 85 degrees, and loaded at any angle. The gun was capable of a higher rate of fire than the gun crews could handle. An experienced crew could maintain a rate of 15 rounds per minute and as many as 22 rounds per minute at ideal loading angles. All U.S. Navy combat vessels that mounted any model of the 5-inch/38 caliber gun carried a 5-inch practice loading machine on which the gun crews drilled constantly to maintain their proficiency. During the 1985–1986 modernization, the practice loader was removed and the gun crews drilled on their actual weapons.

The two basic rounds that the 5-inch MK 12 gun fired were an antiair-

For defense against aircraft and light surface targets, the Missouri *carried twenty 5-inch/38 caliber MK 12 double-purpose guns mounted in 10 twin turrets, arranged with 5 turrets on each side.*

Rendering by Paul Bender

The quadruple 40mm MK 2 gun mount was the standard intermediate-range weapon carried by the Missouri. *Her normal complement was 20 of these mounts, but she operated with a reduced battery during peacetime.*

Rendering by Paul Bender

craft common (AAC) and an HC. The round was semi-fixed with a 54-pound projectile and 28-pound shell case, which included a 15-pound powder charge. A limited number of special purpose illuminating and smoke (WP) projectiles were also carried. Among fuzing combinations that could be used with the AAC rounds was a variable-timed (VT) proximity fuze to detonate the projectile when it came close enough to the target to cause fragment damage.[6] The normal magazine allowance was 500 rounds per gun, plus 40 special types, with 50 rounds per gun stored in the ready-service handling room directly below each turret.

Antiaircraft Battery

The 5-inch/38 caliber guns were double-purpose weapons in that they could be used against aircraft as well as surface targets. In addition to this longer range gun, the U.S. Navy had also developed new intermediate and close range weapons in an effort to throw up a blanket defense against enemy aircraft.

The intermediate range weapon was the 40-mm gun, an adaptation of the Swedish Bofors, which was originally developed in Germany near the end of World War I by Krupp. The gun could be mounted with single-, twin-, and quadruple-barrel arrangements. The standard for the *Iowas* was a quadruple mount, and the *Missouri* carried 20 for a total of 80 barrels. The mounts were distributed along the main deck and in the superstructure to obtain the greatest arcs of fire possible. Each gun was capable of firing a two-pound shell at the rate of 160 rounds per minute. This was one of the more potent weapons of its type in

World War II.

The close-range weapon was the single 20-mm gun, an adaptation of the Swiss Orlikon. It was a free-swinging mount requiring no external power source and could be bolted anywhere. The *Missouri* carried 49 of these mounts located in every area of the main deck, from the very bow to the stern, and they were spotted throughout almost every level of the superstructure. The gun could fire a shell slightly over a quarter of a pound at the rate of 450 rounds per minute.

As the speed of aircraft increased and suicide tactics, such as the

The standard close-in weapon of the Missouri *was the 20mm gun. Shown here is the single 20mm MK 4 gun mount. The* Missouri's *original battery consisted of 49 of these mounts. During most of her commissioned service, however, she carried a mixed battery of single and twin 20mm mounts.*

Rendering by Paul Bender

6. The VT fuze carried a self-contained radio transmitter-receiver. When the projectile came within effective range of the target, an echo of the transmission was reflected back to the receiver causing detonation.

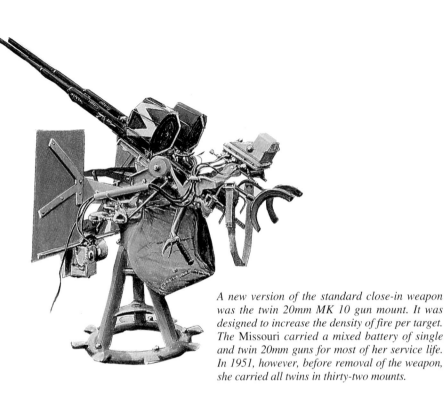

A new version of the standard close-in weapon was the twin 20mm MK 10 gun mount. It was designed to increase the density of fire per target. The Missouri *carried a mixed battery of single and twin 20mm guns for most of her service life. In 1951, however, before removal of the weapon, she carried all twins in thirty-two mounts.*

Rendering by Paul Bender

The new 20mm MK 15 Phalanx CIWS was installed aboard the Missouri *during her 1984–1986 reactivation and modernization. The CIWS was intended as a final defense against anti-ship missiles. The placement of four of these units high in the superstructure provided a full 360-degree target coverage.*

Rendering by Paul Bender

kamikazes, became more commonplace, the 20-mm became less and less effective. Either a heavier shell was required or the density of fire needed to be increased. A heavier weapon would take time to develop, so the BuOrd designed a twin version of the 20-mm to further saturate the antiaircraft pattern. The *Missouri* was fitted with 32 twin mounts that she carried until the end of 1951. Eventually the 20- mm gun was removed from all of the *Iowa* class.

During the *Missouri*'s 1985–1986 modernization, four new 20-mm MK 15 Phalanx CIWS were installed. As a final defense against anti-ship missiles, the four systems provided a full 360 degree target coverage. The weapon was a six-barrel Gatling gun capable of firing 3,000 rounds per minute (six barrels at 500 rounds/minute). The MK 15 used an adaptation of the M61 Vulcan gun used by the Air Force. It fired a MK 149 round, which consisted of a 12.75-mm sub-caliber penetrator; a sabot adapting the penetrator to the 20-mm bore; a pusher that imparted spin to the penetrator; and a 20-mm shell casing. The sabot and pusher were discarded after the round left the muzzle. The penetrator was a heavy metal bullet made of depleted uranium. Its maximum effective range was 2,000 yards.

The Missouri *carried sixteen Harpoon missiles, which gave her an over-the-horizon strike capability against surface targets. The missiles were stored in four quadruple MK 141 Kelvar armored canisters. The harpoon had a range of up to eighty-five miles.*

Rendering by Paul Bender

Missile Battery

The *Missouri* received long-range strike capabilities during her 1986–1986 modernization with the addition of the Harpoon and Tomahawk weapons systems. The Harpoon was an anti-ship missile, and the Tomahawk could be used against both surface and land targets. The Tomahawk also provided the *Missouri* with a nuclear capability.

Two complete Harpoon systems were installed that consisted of four MK 141 launchers and sixteen RGM-84 missiles. Each MK 141 launcher held a cluster of four Kelvar armored canisters in which the missiles were stored and from which they were fired at a fixed angle.

When fired, the booster propelled the missile away from the ship approximately five miles and was discarded. After separation from the booster, the missile's turbojet engine propelled the missile to the target. The stabilizing and actuator fins were stored folded in the canister and would spring out into position after launching. During the flight, the actuator fins received inputs from the

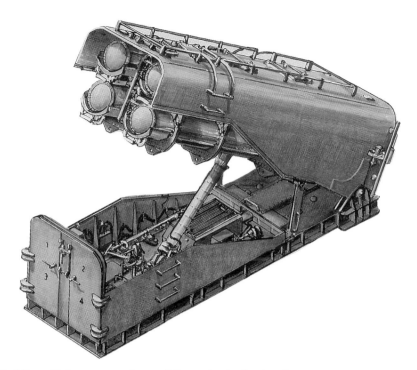

The Missouri*'s long range strike capability against land and surface targets was provided by the BGM-109-series Tomahawk missiles. Thirty-two missiles were carried in eight MK 143 ABLs. The Tomahawk had both conventional and nuclear capabilities against land targets.*

Rendering by Paul Bender

guidance system directing the missile to the target.

Two complete Tomahawk systems consisting of thirty-two BGM-109 series missiles were also installed in eight MK 143 Armored Box Launchers (ABLs). Each ABL held a cluster of four All-Up-Round (AURs) consisting of a canister and the missile. The Tomahawk BGM-109 series had three basic configurations: the Tomahawk Anti-Ship Missile (TASM), the Tomahawk Land-Attack Missile-Conventional (TLAM-C), and the Tomahawk Land-Attack Missile-Nuclear (TLAM-N). The ABL was mounted horizontally with front-end access to the canisters. The canister cluster was attached to the top of the ABL, which was hydraulically raised to the firing position.

When fired, the booster propelled the missile away from the ship approximately eleven miles and was discarded. After separation from the booster, the missile was propelled to the target by its turbofan engine. The missile's wings and actuator fins were stored folded in the canister and sprang out into position after launching. During the flight, the actuator fins received inputs from the guidance system directing the missile to the target.

FIRE CONTROL, RADAR, AND ELECTRONICS

Main Battery

The system to control the fire of the main battery was the MK 38 Gun Fire Control System (GFCS). Two systems were installed consisting of the following primary elements:

* MK 38 directors/rangefinders/radar.
* MK 40 director/optics/radar.
* Turret rangefinders.
* Plotting rooms/system components.
* Spotting aircraft.

When the *Iowa* class was designed, radar was only in the developmental stage and fire control was effected through a system of optical rangefinders, telescopes, periscopes, and spotting glasses in the main battery turrets and directors. The addition of radar greatly enhanced the system because it provided for target acquisition and spotting of shot at night, in fog, through smoke, and all blind firing conditions.

The primary rangefinders were placed in the main battery turrets under the protection of their heavy armor. Long-base (46-foot) rangefinders were incorporated in the after end of each turret. Turret I carried a coincidence rangefinder and Turrets II and III mounted stereoscopic rangefinders.

Two additional long-base (26.5-foot) stereoscopic rangefinders were incorporated in the MK 38 directors and placed aloft atop the forward and after fire control towers. The height of these rangefinders (116 feet forward and 68 feet aft) provided initial ranges at a much greater distance than those in the turrets, however, they could not be nearly as well protected and, therefore, could be brought down more easily as the battle range closed. The fall of shot was spotted from the directors, which provided corrections for the next salvo.

By the time the *Missouri* was completed, fire control radar had advanced considerably, and two MK 8 units were installed, one each atop the forward and aft MK 38 directors. An improved unit, the MK 13, was installed later. These

Rendering by Paul Bender

Gunfire from the main battery was controlled by the MK 38, Mod. 6 director. Range distances were provided by a 26-foot-base rangefinder, and the fall of shot was spotted by the director periscope. The MK 8 radar atop the director provided the same information, making blind firing possible at night or through fog and smoke.

units provided range and bearing information for surface targets and were capable of spotting shell splashes in both range and deflection. Their range was comparable to the maximum effective firing range of the main battery guns.

The MK 40 director was mounted in the roof of the armored conning tower. It consisted of two MK 30 and one MK 32 periscopes mechanically linked together. The MK 30s furnished director train, and the MK 32 was used for spotting. A MK 27 radar set was mounted atop the conning tower for use with the MK 40 director as a standby for the MK 8 and MK 13 sets on the main battery directors. The MK 27 radar was removed when the *Missouri* was placed in mothballs in 1955.

When the *Missouri* was recommissioned in 1986, DR-810 velocimeters were installed on each of the main battery turrets. They were located on the turret roof over the center gun just behind the faceplate. The velocimeter tracked each projectile's flight, providing a quick and accurate assessment of muzzle velocity, which greatly improved the accuracy of subsequent fire. The plotting rooms were located deep within the armored citadel of the ship and housed the remaining vital components of the MK 38 GFCS. One plotting room was located forward on the first platform deck and one was located aft on the third deck. Each contained a MK 8 rangekeeper, a MK 41 stable vertical element, a MK 48 bombardment computer, and a fire control switchboard.

The MK 8 rangekeeper was a mechanical-analog computer into which target motion, own ship's motion, ballistic, and stabilization data were fed. The

target's course and speed were plotted to predict its position when the shells would hit. From this information gun elevation and train orders were generated and relayed to the turrets.

The MK 41 stable vertical was a gimballed gyroscope that measured the roll and pitch of the ship in reference to the line of sight established by the director. This information was fed to the MK 8 rangekeeper for generating the gun orders.

The fire control switchboards controlled all of the inputs and outputs of the various components of the MK 38 GFCS. Through these switchboards, either of the plotting rooms and the various elements of the fire control system could be selectively interchanged.

The ship's aircraft were an important element of the fire control system. In addition to locating the enemy much in advance of when they could be seen from the fire control towers, they spotted the fall of shot and relayed target range information to the ship for correction of following salvos. The aircraft complement for the *Iowa* class was three float planes. There were two catapults located aft, one on each side of the fantail, for launching the aircraft. There was no hangar to house the aircraft, so they were stored either on the catapult in their launching cradle or on deck between the catapults. When commissioned, the *Missouri* carried three OS2U Kingfishers, which were soon replaced by the newer SC-1

The double-purpose 5-inch battery was controlled by the MK 37, Mod. 17 director. Target angles were measured in three positions: range, target bearing, and target elevation. The MK 12/22 radar, mounted above the director, gave the system its blind firing capability. The MK 37 system was very effective against both surface and aerial targets.

Rendering by Paul Bender

In this late 1946 photograph, the Missouri shows little change from her World War II configuration. Her 20mm battery has been reduced to 26 single and 8 twin mounts. Note that two of her Seahawk spotting aircraft are stored on her main deck. The new MK 13 fire control radar has replaced the original MK 8 units atop the MK 38 main battery directors.

Showing changes made during her overhaul a year earlier, the Missouri cruised the Atlantic on 10 March 1949. A new SR-3 air search radar is at the foretop, and a SG-6 is on the foretopmast. Note the tripod mainmast for the new SP air search radar. The 20mm battery now consists of 16 twin mounts. Only two Seahawks are aboard.

Returning from the Far East in April 1951, the Missouri shows changes from her early-1950 refit for Korean service. The unsuccessful SR-3 surface search radar has been replaced by an SR-3c set, which resembled an SPS-6. Her full complement of 32 twin 20mm mounts was installed for the first Korean tour. Note that the rangefinder for turret No. 1 has been removed. The Seahawk spotter aircraft and their catapults have been landed.

These photos of the Missouri *were taken during her shakedown cruise along the East Coast in the summer of 1944. Left: the chain from the fair leader in her bow is the out-haul/inhaul for the minesweeping paravanes. Above and below: the battleship rides at anchor in Casco Bay. The ship just off the bow in the photo below is the battlecruiser* Alaska *(CB-1) also on her shakedown cruise. Note the non-rigid, lighter-than-air patrol blimp over the* Alaska. *The blimps were used extensively for anti-submarine patrols in the Atlantic. The* Missouri *is painted in Measure 32, Design 22D camouflage (see page 61 for details).*

A shakedown cruise is the final test of a ship's readiness to join the fleet. Here are more photos of the Missouri's *1944 summer shakedown. Above left: Captain William Callaghan, the commanding officer, watches an exercise from the bridge while his phone talker, Yoeman 1st class Arthur Colton and the watch officer, Lieutenant Morris Eddy, stand by. Left: an OS 2 U Kingfisher observation plane has just been recovered and is being secured to its launching dolly on the port catapult. Above: a leads man in the chains takes a depth sounding as the battleship enters Casco Bay. Regardless of charts and modern depth reading equipment aboard, the lead line was always a reliable method of sounding in shallow waters.*

Above: the Japanese foreign minister, Mamotu Shigemitsu, stands before his delegation as General MacArthur arranges the surrender document on a table from the crew's mess. The table cloth and chairs were from the officers wardroom. Above right: officers and crewmen gather on the forecastle deck to witness the historic event, which took place on 2 September 1945.

USS MISSOURI (BB-63)
As outfitted July 1944

Camouflage Design: Measure 32,
Design 22D

USS MISSOURI (BB-63)
As outfitted September 1945

Camouflage Design: Measure 22

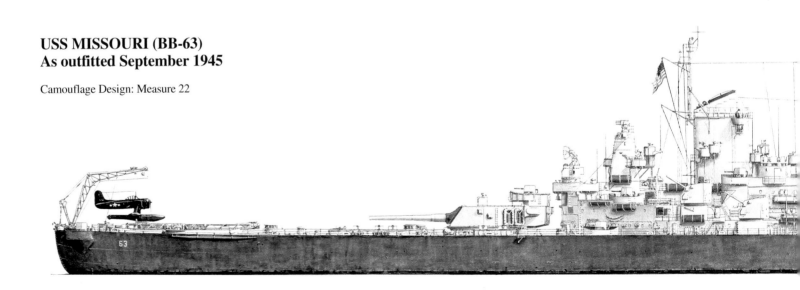

Renderings by Paul Bender

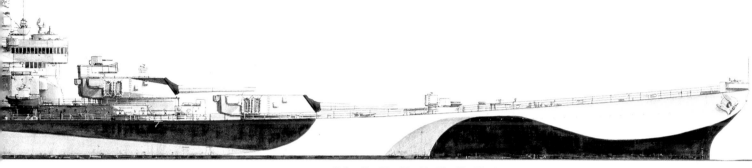

5 0 10 20 30 40 50 60 70 80

scale   feet

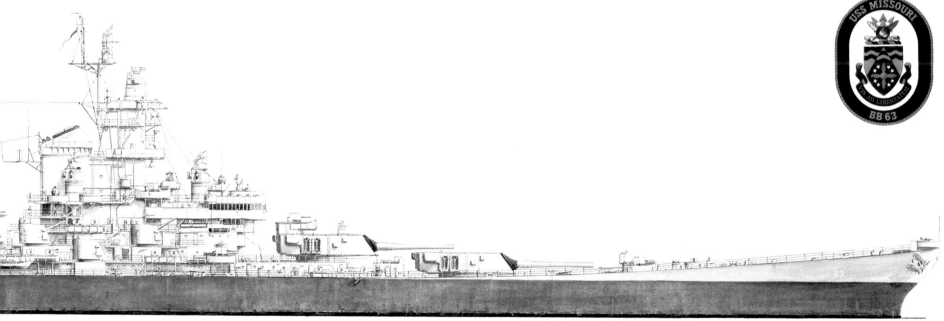

5 0 10 20 30 40 50 60 70 80

scale   feet

USS MISSOURI (BB-63)
As outfitted July 1954

USS MISSOURI (BB-63)
As outfitted July 1986

Renderings by John R. Barrett

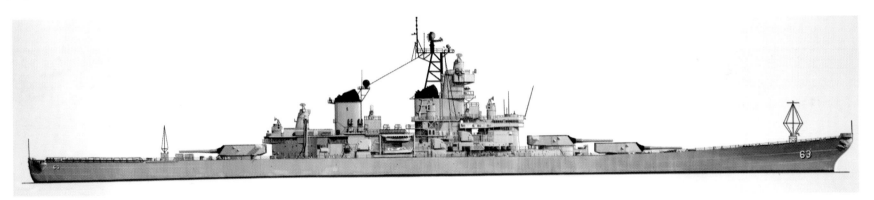

Painting Schedule:

The peacetime painting of U.S. Naval surface vessels is generally referred to as the Haze Gray System. More properly termed Measure US 27, it was derived from the World War II Measure 13. It had the lowest visibility and reflectance over the widest range of light conditions.

Painting Instructions:

Paint all vertical surfaces above the boot topping with No. 27 haze gray (5-H). Paint all decks and other horizontal surfaces, except wood decks, with dark gray deck type A or dark gray non-skid type B. Wood decks are to be natural and uncoated.

The Missouri *rides at anchor off Piraeus, Greece, in April 1946, one of her port calls on a goodwill tour of the Mediterranean. The cruise was also a demonstration of American military power, ready to support Greece and Turkey, who were in danger of being drawn into the Soviet sphere of influence.*

After returning from her first Korean deployment, the Missouri *docks at Pier 7, Norfolk Naval Operating Base, on 27 April 1951. She was the first battleship to reach Korean waters—just one day in advance of the landings at Inchon on 15 September 1950.*

The Missouri *is seen here in the summer of 1986 on her around-the-world shakedown cruise.*

Above and below: the tugs assist the Missouri to her mooring at FOX 5 on Ford Island, 22 June 1998. The wreckage of the Arizona, covered by the Arizona Memorial, lies just ahead at mooring FOX 7. Left: crowds gather aboard the Missouri to celebrate the opening of the ship as a memorial. Note the Arizona Memorial just off the bow of the Missouri and, in the background, the new bridge connecting Ford Island and the main island.

Photo courtesy NcNeil Wilson Communications, Inc., Honolulu.

Seahawk. The U.S. Navy continued to use spotter aircraft after World War II, and the *Missouri* carried two Seahawks as late as 1948 when they and their catapults were landed and replaced by helicopters.

After modernization in 1986, the *Missouri* received the first aircraft she had carried since her Seahawks were landed in 1948. The aircraft was the Pioneer Remotely-Piloted Vehicle (RPV). The Pioneer system consisted of a ground control station on the ship, two portable control stations, and eight RPVs. The system missions were reconnaissance, surveillance, search and rescue, weapons targeting, and battle damage assessment.

Secondary Battery

The MK 37 director was designed to control the 5-inch/38 caliber double purpose guns against either air or surface targets, and to provide illumination control for star shells and searchlights. The MK 37 GFCS was a linear-rate system in many respects similar to the main battery system described above. It measured target position in three coordinates: range, relative target bearing, and target elevation. The three major components of the system were a director with radar, a stable element, and a computer with associated instruments at the gun. The *Missouri* had four MK 37 systems.

The directors were located as high as practicable in the superstructure to give the best target coverage possible. One was located on top of the pilot house overlooking the conning tower, one was atop the end of the after superstructure, and one was located on each side of the forward stack at the approximate level of the forward unit. The computers and stable elements were located in the plotting rooms adjacent to the main battery plotting rooms.

The director was equipped with a stereoscopic rangefinder (15-foot base), two telescopes, and a slewing sight. The control officer could rapidly designate a target and bring it into the field of the optics with the slewing sight. The *Missouri* carried a MK 12/22 radar antenna atop each director house. The antennas were aligned with the director optics, and either could be used alone, or in combination, thus providing optimum tracking accuracy. During the *Missouri*'s 1948 refit, the MK 12/22 antenna was replaced with the newer, more accurate MK 25 antenna.

In the plotting rooms, the stable element established a horizontal reference plane through use of a gyroscope, so that level and crosslevel could be measured. This information was fed to the adjacent computer, which made the calculations required for control of the double-purpose battery. The result was in turn relayed to the director to maintain the line of sight to the target and as gun orders to the gun mounts for aiming the guns.

Embarking midshipmen and Naval Reservists for a summer training cruise, the Missouri *is anchored in the Chesapeake Bay off Annapolis, Maryland, in this 6 June 1953 photograph. Soot blowing is underway obscuring most of the forward radar and electronics gear. On the after stack, a tripod mast has been erected to support the new SP air search set on the maintop. On the maintopmast is the SG surface search radar, and just visible through the smoke is a new SG-6 set on the foretopmast.*

Antiaircraft Battery

The simple lightweight MK 51 director was developed for control of the 40-mm power-driven gun mount. The MK 51 was a relative-rate system incorporating the MK 14 gunsight. Directors were located near the gun mounts they controlled, usually just above the mount to be relatively free from its vibration and smoke. Photographs indicate that an additional fire control system, the MK 57, apparently was added during the November-December 1944 refit at Hunters Point. It could control a group of 40-mm mounts from a remote location and, with its integral radar equipment, was capable of being used for blind firing. Ring sights and hand-cranks were also mounted on the 40-mm gun mounts for manually pointing, training, and firing the guns.

The 20-mm free-swinging gun mount was equipped with a ring sight for aiming and pointing. Training was effected by the operator's body movement through a set of handle bars and shoulder rests. It was necessary for the operator to lead the target in both traverse and elevation. Usually, every fifth round in the belt was a tracer, which assisted the operator in spotting his fire. Using a lead-angle computing mechanism, the MK 14 gun sight controlled antiaircraft machine guns against rapidly moving targets at short ranges. The sight could be mounted

In this mid-1954 photograph, the Missouri *displays her final configuration before being placed in reserve. A quadrapod mainmast has been installed to carry the weight of a new SPS-8 air search set, which replaced the SP unit. The SG surface search set has not been put back. All of the 20mm guns were removed by April 1952.*

on either the single or twin 20-mm mounts and, as mentioned above, was the primary element of the MK 51 director.

The MK 15, 20-mm Phalanx installed during the *Missouri*'s 1985–1986 modernization was controlled by the AN/VPS-2 pulsed, doppler-type search and track radar. It tracked the target and the outgoing rounds and corrected for the angular difference between them. When in fully automatic, the system would search, track, fire, kill assess, and return to search. The original system had no Identification Friend or Foe (IFF), and any high-speed, incoming target was engaged. IFF was later developed and retrofitted to the systems.

Missile Battery

The RGM-84 Harpoon and BGM-109, TSAM Tomahawk weapons control systems were similar, both using active radar for homing in on targets. Both of the TLAM series Tomahawk missiles used inertial guidance and were targeted by Terrain Contour Matching (TERCOM).

Search Radar

When the *Missouri* was completed, her radar suit consisted of the new SK-2 and two SG sets. The SK-2 was mounted on the foretop. One SG set was placed atop the foretopmast, and the second unit was installed atop the pole mainmast.

Long range aircraft detection was provided by the SK-2 air search set. Its 17-foot dish antenna had a range of 100 nm and a height capability of 10,000 feet at that range.

Ship detection was furnished by the two SG surface search sets. A small waveguide-fed unit, SG could detect large ships at over 20 nm and aircraft under 500 feet at about 15 nm. Its displays of vessels, as well as land masses, made it useful to navigation.

In her 1948 refit, the *Missouri* received the new SR-3 air search radar, which replaced the SK-2. The new set proved unsatisfactory, falling far short of the SK-2 in range. When the ship was refitted for Korean service, the SR-3 was replaced with an improved unit, the SR-3c, which was similar to the SPS-6. The *Missouri* went into reserve with this set.

Also during the 1948 refit, the *Missouri* received an SP air search radar. To mount the SP, a new tripod mainmast was fitted on the after stack, replacing the pole. The new antenna was installed on the maintop. During this availability period, she also received an SG-6, replacing the SG on her foretopmast. The aft SG was placed on a new maintopmast.

The last change to the *Missouri*'s radar suit before she was placed in the Reserve Fleet was in 1953 when the SPS-8 set replaced the SP. The new antenna was much heavier than its predecessor and required a new mainmast arrangement. A quadrapod mast was fitted with its after main legs extending down to the superstructure. Its forward legs were supported by the after stack. The SPS-8 was installed on a new maintop. A new maintopmast was also fitted, but the SG set was not put back.

When modernized during 1985–1986, the *Missouri* received the latest in search radar: SPS 10 and SPS 49. A heavy new tripod foremast was fitted to accommodate these antennas and other electronic gear. The SPS 10 was an older, but still reliable surface search set, which could effectively range to the horizon.

The SPS 49 was the most effective air search set in use by the U.S. Navy and had features for use with Electronic Counter-Counter Measures (ECCM) and Automatic Detection and Tracking (ADT).

Electronics

The *Missouri* was outfitted with a MK III IFF system when completed. The system was capable of identifying radar contacts and could furnish its identity to challenging signals with its interrogator and transponder units.

The BM interrogator sent out a coded signal. If the signal was received by a friendly contact, it activated a transponder unit in the contact, which sent out a favorable return signal. The antenna for the BM was mounted on the SK-2 antenna frame. Both signals were sent out and received together but were displayed separately. The BM antenna was the protruding dipole in the center of the SK-2 dish.

The BK transponder unit was activated by a signal from an interrogator and returned a favorable signal, as indicated previously. An unfriendly unit would be unable to respond with the proper signal and/or on the required frequency. The BK antenna resembled a "ski pole" and was placed as high as possible to avoid obstructions.

Electronic Counter Measures

From photographs taken in late 1945, it appears that the *Missouri* was fitted with two Electronic Counter Measure (ECM) systems: a direct noise amplifier and a jammer.

Elements of a direct noise amplifier system included two AS-56 type dipole antennas, one on each side of the foretop, and four AS-37 "wagon wheel" and dipole antennas, one each to port and starboard and fore and aft of the air defense station. The noise was a continuous output and appeared as "grass" on the enemy's display.

A standard TDY jamming unit was on a platform on the forward end of the fire control tower just below the air defense station. Two DBM antennas were located just forward of the two "wagon wheel" antennas on the sides of the air defense station. Jamming was produced by the TDY unit in conjunction with the DBM antennas. The DBMs furnished signal information to the TDY, which sent out a masking signal in the direction of the incoming pulse, thus jamming the returning signal rendering it illegible.

When modernized, the *Missouri* received the latest ECM gear, including the SLQ 32(V)3 and eight Super Rapid Blooming Offboard Chaff (SRBOC) launchers. The quick-reaction mode of the SLQ 32 could initiate jamming and launch SRBOC decoys against targets that appeared suddenly. Also installed was the SLQ NIXIE, a towed device designed to replace the ship as a target for torpedoes.

Some of the radar and electronics equipment installed aboard the Missouri *during her reactivation and modernization are shown here. On the new foretop are the search radars, SPS 10 (small) and SPS 49 (large). A portion of the MK II AIMS IFF system is visible on the foremast. Shown below and to each side of the MK 13 main battery fire control antenna are the SQL-32 ECM antennas. On the forward end of the air defense level is an OE-8 satellite communications antenna. The inboard and outboard whip antennas at the bridge are the receivers and transmitter antennas of the AS-2537A/SR system.*

Above: this aerial view of the Missouri *taken in November 1986 during her around-the-world shakedown cruise shows the full range of her weapons, fire control, radar, and electronics. Just forward of the second stack, note the round globe-like structure that houses the radar antenna for controlling the RPVs. The boats were subject to blast damage, and turret No. 3 was restricted to firing only to starboard during peacetime operations. During Desert Storm, however, they were landed to give turret No. 3 her full range of operation. Below:* the Missouri is shown in the Persian Gulf on 12 January 1991 during operation Desert Storm. An Iraqi mine, one of the ever present dangers, floats near the battleship prior to being detonated by an Explosive Ordnance Disposal (EOD) team. Note that a second antenna for controlling the RPVs has been added just below the air defense level forward.*

The Missouri *lies at anchor off Bayonne, New Jersey, in August 1944. This aerial broadside clearly shows the large area that had to be protected. The armor citadel of the vessel ranged from just forward of turret No. 1 to just aft of turret No. 3. A shell approaching at* this angle would be close to the far side of the immune zone and might penetrate some of the deck armor, but because of the inclination of the side armor, the shell would probably glance off the main belt.

PROTECTION

Armor Protection

Heavy armor provided protection against gunfire. Contrary to popular belief, protection was not related to the armor's thickness, but its effectiveness within a specified immune zone. The immune zone had an inner edge that marked the shortest range at which the side and deck armor could not be penetrated, and an outer edge that marked the shortest range at which plunging fire would penetrate the deck armor. In theory, immunity was desired against a specific weapon, usually the main armament of the vessel itself, because it would overpower a weaker adversary and avoid contact with a more powerful one. If engagement with a more powerful adversary could not be avoided, the rule for the action would be to maneuver into a range where the ship's weapons would be the most effective against the attacker's armor. A difficult situation but clearly the only chance of survival. The size of the zone was determined by the expected, or preferred, battle ranges, which were normally the greatest distance at which the main battery could be effectively managed by the fire control system. The thickness and configuration of the armor was designed to suit these conditions.

The armor protection of the *Iowa* class was designed to resist a 2,240-pound 16-inch/45 caliber shell fired from a distance between 18,000 and 30,000 yards. In June 1939, a year after the *Iowa* design had been fixed, a new 2,700-pound shell was adopted. The new and more powerful shell caused the ship's immune zone to shrink to between 20,200 and 25,500 yards. Progress on the first two ships had advanced to the point where armor had already been ordered. There was no hope of any extensive revision to the armor protection system. Some minor improvements, however, were possible in the *Missouri* and subsequent ships of the class.

The armor protection of a battleship can be visualized as an armored box, or citadel, into which all of the vital equipment, such as machinery, magazines, plotting rooms, etc., necessary for survival, was fitted. Its usual length was from the forward end of the first turret's barbette to the after end of the barbette for the last turret. Items outside the box requiring armor protection, such as turrets, conning tower, fire control directors, and steering gear, were connected to the box forming a sort of appendage.

The armor used in the construction of the *Missouri* and the other *Iowa* class battleships, consisted of three types:

1. Class A armor had a hard, non-ductile face and a ductile back. The purpose of the hard face was to break up the attacking projectile and the soft back was designed to prevent the plate from shattering. It was superior in penetration resistance to all other types of armor.

2. Class B armor was substantially uniform in composition and physical properties. Often referred to as homogenous armor, it relied on its strength and ductility by spreading the force of impact over a wider area.

3. Special treatment steel (STS) armor was Class B armor that was used in ships structures for added protection not provided by mild steel.

4. Cast armor was cast directly in its final shape and was usually homogenous but could be face hardened. It was useful in fabricating small housings, such as rangerfinders and sight hoods.

These two photographs show the installation of the Class B lower belt armor. Each plate is approximately ten feet across the top and twenty-eight feet deep. Note the vertical keys and key ways for aligning the individual plates and the scalloped butt straps joining the plates. The Class A upper belt plates, which were approximately thirty feet across at the top and ten feet deep, were aligned using the key way on the top of the lower belt plates. Note the outboard nineteen-degree slope of the armor belt.

No.1 barbette to frame 166 aft of No. 3 barbette. The main portion of the belt, or upper belt, was Class A armor 12.2 inches thick extending from a lip just above the second deck to a lip just below the third deck. The secondary portion of the belt was Class B armor extending down from the lower lip of the upper belt to the inner bottom and was tapered from 12.2 inches to 1.4 inches. The 12.2 inches of armor, which sloped at 19 degrees, was considered equivalent to 13.5 inches of vertical armor. Extending the armor down to the inner bottom was intended to protect against shells falling short and continuing under water. A portion of the main belt was continued aft to protect the steering gear leads.

The ends of the box were closed by Class A armored transverse bulkheads. As originally designed, these bulkheads were 11.3 inches thick and the *Iowa* and *New Jersey* were so completed. When the *Missouri* and subsequent ships of the class were ordered, treaty weight restrictions were no longer in effect, and these bulkheads were increased to 14.5 inches for added protection at a wider range of target angles.

Heavy plate armor, such as Class A and Class B, was formed by either forging or rolling. Plates less than 4 inches thick were rolled in a mill while plates over 4 inches were forged. In this discussion, armor less than 4 inches thick is referred to as STS plate.

The design of the armor protection system was essentially the same as for the *South Dakota* class. The side, or belt armor, was inclined to 19 degrees and hung on the outboard side of No. 3 torpedo bulkhead from frame 50 forward of

The top of the box was covered with a system of armored decks, which included protection against aerial bombs. The main deck was designated the bomb deck, the second deck was the main armor deck, and the splinter deck was a flat fitted just below the second deck only for the length of the box. The bomb deck was 1.5-inch STS, the main armor deck was 4.75-inch Class B armor laid on 1.25-inch STS, and the splinter deck was .625-inch STS. Within the immune zone, the main armor deck was designed to defeat plunging shells, which entered the side above the top of the main belt. The splinter deck was intended to catch any spall and pieces of armor that might be broken off. If the angle of fall was steep enough, there would be the added protection of the armor on the bomb deck. The bomb deck was designed to detonate general purpose bombs on contact and arm armor piercing bombs so they would explode between the bomb deck and the main armor deck.

New ballistic plating was added to several spaces when the *Missouri* was modernized in 1985–1986. The newly plated areas were in the superstructure and included the new Combat Engagement Center (CEC) and Tomahawk, Harpoon, and CIWS support spaces. (For details and thickness of armor for the conning tower, turrets, etc., see General Data Table.)

Underwater Protection

Protection against the effects of torpedoes, mines, and near miss bombs was provided by the side protective and triple-bottom systems. Both systems were multilayered and intended to absorb the energy from an underwater explosion equivalent to a 700-pound charge of TNT. The size of this charge was determined from information obtained in an intelligence survey from the mid-1930s, and when the *Iowa* class was designed, the U.S. Navy was unaware of the advances the Japanese had made in torpedo technology. One of the early unpleasant surprises of the Pacific War was the Japanese 24-inch "long lance" torpedo carried by most of their surface craft. The Japanese were able to pack a considerably larger explosive charge, by U.S. standards, into their aerial and submarine torpedoes.

The side protection system consisted of four tanks on the outboard side of the hull. They extended from the third deck to the turn of the bilge. The tanks were inclined 19 degrees, the same as the armor belt, which was attached to the third torpedo bulkhead inboard. The full tank system ranged from frame 50 forward of No. 1 barbette to frame 166 aft of No. 3 barbette, which was essentially the length of the armored box, or citadel. The two outboard tanks were liquid-loaded with fuel oil or ballast, and the two inboard tanks were kept void. In theory, the liquid layers would absorb the shock from an explosion and contain most of the shards from the damaged structure. The first void was expected to contain any leakage, and the belt on its inboard side was intended to stop any fragments that penetrated the second torpedo bulkhead. The designers hoped that this system would keep the second void and fourth torpedo, or holding, bulkhead intact pro-

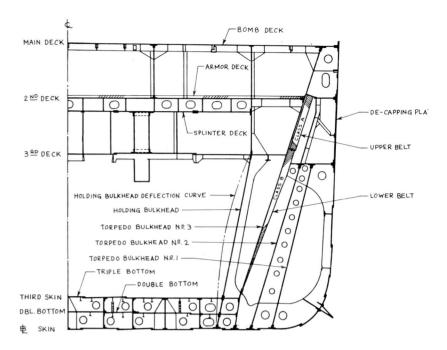

This sketch of the midship section of the Missouri *shows the arrangement of armor, torpedo defense, and triple-bottom systems as described in the text. Note the de-capping plate on the shell between the second and third decks. It was 1 1/2 inches thick and had enough resistance to start the time delay of a base detonating type fuze. If it dislodged or knocked off the armor piercing cap of a projectile, the resistance of the main belt was considerably increased.*

tecting the machinery and magazine spaces. The system was shallowest at No. 1 and No. 3 barbettes, a consequence of the fineness of the hull form, but this defect had to be accepted, because any increase in hull volume, especially around the forward barbette, would have resulted in a reduction of speed.

The triple-bottom system consisted of two layers of tanks on the very bottom of the hull between the holding bulkheads of the side protection system. The tanks were formed by the shell at the bottom of the hull and the inner-bottom and third-bottom flats. The inner bottom ran the entire length of the ship, but the third bottom was spread essentially under the vitals of the ship, from frame 36 well forward of No.1 barbette to frame 173 well aft of No. 3 barbette. The double-bottom tanks were liquid-loaded with fuel oil and reserve feed and potable water, except near the ends where they were kept void. The third-bottom tanks were all kept void. In theory, the system was intended to absorb the shock of an underwater explosion and function much the same as the side protection system.

Left: the general arrangement of the rudders and propellers is shown in this photograph of the Missouri taken in dry dock at the New York Navy Yard on 23 July 1944. The propellers converted the 212,000 shaft horsepower into thrust. Note the five-bladed inboard propellers and the four-bladed outboard propellers. The two semi-balanced streamlined-type rudders were located slightly inboard of the center of the propellers to take advantage of the flow of water through the tunnel stern and the wash from the propellers.

Opposite, the Iowas had eight boilers that produced high pressure, superheated steam to four sets of geared turbines that drove the shafts. This view shows boiler No. 6 in boiler room No. 3. Boiler No. 5 is located on the opposite side of the room. Note the burners and the gear to control the operation of the boiler.

ENGINEERING

The *Missouri* and her sisters of the *Iowa* class were the fastest battleships ever built. Their machinery was designed for extreme performance to produce the specified 33-knot speed at full load displacement, a performance that required a total of 212,000 shaft horsepower. Enormous fuel storage capacity enabled them to easily meet their required endurance of 15,000 nautical miles at 15 knots.

About one-third of the ship, in hull volume, was devoted to engineering areas containing the main engines, boilers, generators, evaporators, air compressors, steering engines, anchor windlass, deck winches, repair lockers, etc., which were operated by and/or maintained by the engineering department.

Propulsion

The design and weight of the propulsion machinery arrangement was dependent on the disposition of the units within the hull. The propulsion machinery was distributed in an alternating fire room, engine room arrangement and the location of the propellers was fixed by the design of the hull form. The first step, therefore, was the location of the main engines and the run of the propeller shafts. The rest of the machinery, in both the fire rooms and engine rooms, could then be located to accommodate the shafting. Two auxiliary machinery spaces, one forward and one aft of the main spaces, housed the units not directly associated with the propulsion machinery.

Steam for the plant was furnished by eight boilers and delivered to four sets of geared turbines, which were direct-coupled to double-reduction gears that drove the shafts. The main steam system was divided into two groups; the forward group consisting of fire rooms No. 1 and No. 2 and engine rooms No. 1 and No. 2, and the after group consisting of fire rooms No. 3 and No. 4 and engine rooms No. 3 and No. 4. Although the main steam could not be cross-connected between the two groups, each space could be cross-connected within its group.

The boilers were the three-drum, double-furnace, express-type that generated steam at 565 psi and 850 degrees F. The turbine group consisted of one high-pressure turbine, one low-pressure turbine, and one double-reduction gear. The high-pressure turbine was coupled to the high-speed, high-pressure pinion, and the low-pressure turbine was coupled to the high-speed, low-pressure pinion of the reduction gear. The low-pressure turbine contained an astern element in each end, which could reverse the shaft rotation for backing down. The reduction gear reduced the high-speed input from the turbines in two stages furnishing 202 rpm to the shafts to make 33 knots. All ancillary machinery for the main plant was in the same space as the equipment it served.

One of the improvements to the main propulsion plant during the *Missouri*'s 1985–1986 modernization was the conversion of the boilers to burn standard navy distillate fuel. The fuel oil storage and transfer system was also overhauled to handle the new fuel.

Auxiliaries

The electrical plant included eight 1,250-kw steam turbo-generators, which furnished power to the hundreds of electrical motors that operated the ordnance, fire control, radar, and electronics equipment, as well as the ship's hotel load. There were also two 250 kw emergency diesel generators, which could furnish power if any or all of the ship's service generators failed.

Each machinery room had two turbo-generators adjacent to the main engines and steam supply. The emergency diesel generators were in auxiliary machinery rooms, one forward and one aft of the main propulsion rooms. The forward auxiliary machinery room also contained the distilling plant. Three large triple-effect evaporators processed sea water into feed water for the boilers and potable water for drinking, cooking, and personal cleaning. When at sea, the boilers had priority over any other uses.

During the *Missouri*'s 1985-1986 modernization, 400 Hz power was added to operate the new electronics equipment and the NTDS. The equipment consisted of three 100 kW solid-state frequency converters installed in a former radio area aft on barbette No. 2.

An important support system installed during modernization was the sewage CHT system, which prevented the discharge of sewage into rivers, harbors, and coastal waters. (For details and data for the engineering plant, see General Data Table.)

Damage Control

Damage control encompassed all efforts directed toward keeping a ship in action despite the effects of any damage that may be sustained not only from combat but from non-battle damage such as fire, collision, grounding, weather damage, and explosion as well.

The engineering department was responsible for the organization and administration of damage control practices and procedures, which included two separate, but related functions:

1. Damage control was concerned with the preservation of stability and watertight integrity, the control of fires and flooding, the repair of structural damage, and the control of Nuclear, Biological and Chemical (NBC) contamination.

2. Engineering casualty control was concerned with the effects of operational and battle casualties to the ship's machinery and related systems.

Damage Control Central (DCC), located on the third deck forward of the machinery spaces near the centerline of the ship, exercised control over all repair parties and the main engine control station. Each of seven repair parties was assigned a specific area of responsibility manning lockers strategically located throughout the ship, a battle dressing station, and a personnel decontamination station. Main Engine Control was located with the after engine group in engine room No. 3.

DCC contained a set of Damage Control Diagrams and numerous lighted status panels that indicated the various engineering and liquid loading conditions of the ship. Damage was plotted on the diagrams to establish the extent of any damage and determine what corrective measures should be taken. Each repair locker also contained a set of Damage Control Diagrams so that damage could be plotted concurrently with DCC. Typical damage control equipment stored in the repair lockers included access tools for forcible entry, cutting torches, patching kits for broken piping, plugging and patching kits for structural repairs, shoring materials to reinforce weakened structures, an electrical repair kit, and radiological defense equipment.

The importance of damage control cannot be over-stated. When damage occurred, the survivability of a ship could well depend on the quick and effective efforts of the damage control team.

HISTORY

The last battleship launched by the United States, the USS *Missouri* (BB 63) was built by the New York Navy Yard, Brooklyn, N.Y. Her keel was laid on 6 January 1941, and she was launched 29 January 1944 under the sponsorship of Margaret Truman. Her father, then a senior U.S. Senator from *Missouri*, spoke at the ceremonies.

"The time is surely coming when the people of *Missouri* can thrill with pride as the *Missouri* and her sister ships, with batteries blazing, sail into Tokyo Bay," said Senator Truman.

His words were prophetic. That winter's day, none could have imagined the crucial part both he and the warship would play in bringing the war in the Pacific to its conclusion. Commissioned 11 June 1944, the *Missouri* spent her first summer and fall along the East Coast. Finally in November, she received the orders that sent her into the Pacific war zone.

By the end of January 1945, she was screenin the *Lexington*'s fast carrier task force, which was headed for the first air strikes against the Japanese mainland since Doolittle's bombing raid launched from the carrier *Hornet* in 1942. Underway on 10 February, with Task Force 58, the battleship launched its three SC-1 Seahawks and almost immediately, one of the float planes was in trouble. It crashed into the sea within 10,000 yards of the *Missouri* and the destroyer *Lewis Hancock* moved in to rescue the pilot. Despite the rescuers best efforts, the injured and unconscious pilot, Lieutenant Everett N. Frothingham, slipped from their harness and was never seen again.

As U.S. Marines fought their way ashore on Iwo Jima on 19 February, the *Missouri* covered the fast carriers of Task Group 58.2 as they launched air strikes to support the landings. The approach of evening brought an enemy bomber headed in on her port beam. At about 9,800 yards, the crews on the *Missouri*'s 5-inch guns opened fire and within seconds, sent it plunging seaward. Leaving Iwo, the *Missouri* screened the carriers of Task Force 58 for strikes against Tokyo, but severe weather put an abrupt end to the attack. In March, she joined the *Wisconsin*, and the cruisers *Alaska* and *Guam* to make up the fast-moving Task Group 58.4. Screening the carriers as they sent their planes aloft for strikes along the coast of Japan's Inland Sea, the *Missouri* brought down four enemy raiders on 14 March 1945. The guns of the *Missouri* were again trained on

Above: the Missouri *was launched at the New York Navy Yard on 29 January 1944. It was sponsored by Margaret Truman, daughter of the senior U.S. Senator from Missouri, Harry S. Truman. Note the fine lines of her distinctive bow.*

Left: on 11 June 1944, Captain William M. Callaghan read his orders and placed the USS Missouri *(BB63) in commission. During the brief ceremony at the New York Navy Yard, the band played the national anthem followed by "Anchors Aweigh."*

the skies as their carrier group came under fierce kamikaze attacks on 18 and 19 March during which the carriers *Enterprise* and *Franklin* were hit. Meanwhile, carrier aircraft had already begun pre- invasion attacks on Okinawa, and on 24 March the *Missouri*, *Wisconsin*, and *New Jersey*, moved in to loose their firepower on the island's fortifications. Firing 180 rounds that day, the *Missouri*'s 16-inch guns damaged or destroyed several buildings, gun emplacements, and an ammunition dump along the southeast coast of the island.

The American forces finally stormed ashore on Okinawa on the morning of 1 April 1945, with air support from carriers guarded by the *Missouri* and her sister warships. She was screening the carriers involved in air strikes on the island on the afternoon of 11 April 1945, when an enemy suicide plane came in low to starboard, headed, it seemed, for the battleship's bridge. At 1443, the seriously damaged plane struck three feet below main deck level. Shattered pieces of the plane spread along her starboard side. The pilot's body was cut in half by the crash, the top half landing on the main deck with enough force to destroy a floater net stowage basket. One of the plane's machine guns became embedded in the barrel of a 40-mm gun. A wing hit in the area of the center 5-inch gun mount. The resulting gasoline fire was quickly extinguished, and all other damage was superficial. Later that same day, the *Missouri*'s gunners brought down another would-be suicide and a twin-engine bomber.

For twelve hours on 16 April 1945, the *Missouri* was under almost constant attack. That afternoon, she opened fire on a low-flying plane that crashed close aboard the carrier *Intrepid*. Just two minutes later, a second plane came in from the north. Though his plane had received multiple hits, the pilot made a desperate attempt to crash the *Missouri*. The wing of the enemy plane clipped the *Missouri*'s stern crane before crashing a short distance astern where it exploded violently. Debris was thrown on board the battleship, but she sustained very little damage. Almost immediately, a third enemy plane dove on the ship from her port quarter. It burst into flames and passed over her at about 300 feet, crashing just off her starboard bow. With deadly accuracy the guns of the *Missouri* brought down two more planes. During the same afternoon attack, two of the battleship's men were wounded by shrapnel and strafing. That night, the *Missouri*'s gunners helped to repel two enemy air raids.

In all, during the Okinawa campaign, the *Missouri* shot down five enemy planes, scored one probable kill, and assisted in the destruction of six other attackers. She helped to repel twelve daylight enemy air attacks and four night raids.

On 18 May 1945, the *Missouri* became the flagship of Admiral William F. Halsey, Jr., USN, Commander Third Fleet. The *Missouri* proceeded on 2 and 3 June 1945 to lead the Third Fleet for strikes against airfields and installations on Kyushu, Japan. On the way, she rode out a fierce storm suffering only slight damage to some of her topside fittings. She was ready for a second strike against Kyushu on 8 June and then, retired to Leyte in the Philippine Islands.

During the Okinawa campaign, the Missouri *was crashed by a damaged suicide plane the afternoon of 11 April 1945. Striking just below the main deck level at the after end of the superstructure, the plane strewed wreckage all along the starboard side. The photograph above shows the plane just before impact, and the one below indicates some of the wreckage.*

On their way to Tokyo Bay and the Japanese surrender, the Missouri, *left, and* Iowa *transfer personnel, mail, and movies. It was a rare sight to see two battleships so close and under way. There are many differences in detail and outfitting that become apparent when comparing the two ships.*

Flagship of the U.S. Third Fleet, the Missouri *rides at anchor in Sagami Wan on 27 August 1945 preparing to enter Tokyo Bay for the Japanese surrender ceremony.*

Leaving the Philippines on 1 July, the *Missouri* led the Third Fleet into the enemy's home waters on 8 July. The Fleet's air raids took Tokyo by surprise on 10 July with a devastating attack repeated up and down the coast of Japan. For the first time, a naval force had brought destruction to major installations within the home islands of Japan. During the attacks, the *Missouri* took part in Task Force 38's bombardment of the Nihon Steel Company and Wanishi Ironworks at Muroran on Hokkaido, expending 297 rounds of 16-inch ammunition. During the night of 17–18 July, she bombarded industrial targets in the Hitachi area of Honshu and ended the month screening carrier strikes against Tokyo. In the month-long attack, the Third Fleet had gained control of the sea and air approaches to Japan's main islands.

On 9 August, the day the second atomic bomb was dropped, the *Missouri* and Task Force 38 continued to pound Hokkaido and Northern Honshu. That day was the battleship's last encounter with enemy planes. At 0745 on 15 August 1945, word reached the fleet that Japan had surrendered. At 1109,

Admiral Halsey ordered the whistle and siren to sound as the battle colors were broken at the mainmast. His personal flag was then hoisted at the foremast, recognizing the end of four years, eight months, and seven days of war with Japan. As the Task Force retired to the southeast, several unreconstructed or poorly informed Japanese pilots attacked the formation and were shot down by the outer combat air patrol.

On the morning of 29 August 1945, the *Missouri* entered Tokyo Bay to drop anchor in Berth F-71 to prepare for the formal surrender ceremony scheduled to take place on her deck. Dawn of 2 September 1945 found the *Missouri*'s decks astir with preparations. By 0730, a destroyer had deposited 170 newsmen, cameramen, and other media aboard and they were soon followed by representatives of all the allied powers. Next came Fleet Admiral Chester W. Nimitz; General of the Army, Douglas MacArthur; and the Japanese representatives headed by their Foreign Minister Mamoru Shigemitsu. At 0902, General MacArthur stepped before the battery of microphones to begin the worldwide broadcast of the surrender ceremony. It was all over in exactly 23 minutes and by 0930, as a flight of Army Air Force B-29 bombers passed overhead, the Japanese emissaries were leaving the ship.

Admiral Nimitz, who had directed the naval war in the Pacific, had a special message for his Fleet, which read in part:

"On board all naval vessels at sea and in port, and at our many island bases in the Pacific, there is rejoicing and thanksgiving. The long and bitter struggle, which Japan started so treacherously on the 7th of December 1941, is at an end …Today all freedom-loving peoples of the world rejoice in the victory …We also pay tribute to those who defended our freedom at the cost of their lives …To them we have a solemn obligation …to insure that their sacrifice will help to make this a better and safer world in which to live …"

With war behind her, the *Missouri* left Tokyo Bay on 6 September 1945 and headed for New York where she became the flagship of Admiral Jonas Ingram, Commander in Chief, United States Atlantic Fleet on 24 October 1945. After overhaul in the New York Navy Yard, the *Missouri* was on her way in March, 1946 to the Mediterranean. Her goodwill mission was also an impressive demonstration of American military power, symbolizing U.S. support for Greece and Turkey, who were in danger of being drawn into the Soviet orbit of satellite states.

On 19 August 1946, President Truman gave the go-ahead for deployment of a strong fleet to the eastern Mediterranean, noting as he did so, "We might as well find out whether the Russians are bent on world conquest now as in five or ten years." The American naval strength continued to grow, maintaining the precarious balance of power in the Mediterranean.

In Rio de Janeiro, on 2 September 1947, the *Missouri* provided the site for President Truman to sign the Rio Treaty making the Monroe Doctrine a multilateral pact. Business and ceremonial duties concluded, President Truman, accom-

The Missouri *is anchored in Tokyo Bay, and the crew stands at quarters awaiting the arrival of Allied and Japanese representatives for the formal surrender of Japan.*

panied by Mrs. Truman and their daughter Margaret, returned to the United States aboard the battleship. An overhaul at the New York Navy Yard took the *Missouri* into 1948, followed by a midshipmen training cruise to Portugal, France, Algeria, and Cuba. On 17 January 1950, she attracted unwanted attention on her departure from Hampton Roads. She was 1.6 miles off Thimble Shoals Light when she went aground. Lifted about seven feet above waterline, she stuck hard and fast until a small fleet of tugs, with the help of pontoons, and an incoming tide, freed her on 1 February.

Above: Admiral Nimitz and General MacArthur, followed by Admiral Halsey, take their positions for the formal ceremony that ended World War II in the Pacific. Above right: the Japanese delegation arrives and General MacArthur invites them to take their places for the ceremony. Right, the commemorative plaque that was placed on the spot where the table stood upon which the surrender was signed.

Above: the Japanese foreign minister, Mamotu Shigemitsu, signs the "Instrument of Surrender." As other high ranking Allied officers look on, General MacArthur announces the momentous events taking place. Above right: other Japanese emissaries sign the surrender documents. On the bulkhead behind them is Commodore Matthew C. Perry's flag, the first United States flag to fly over Japan. Right: Admiral Nimitz signs the surrender documents as General MacArthur, Admiral Halsey, and Rear Admiral Forrest Sherman watch. The flag, table, table cloth, replicas of the surrender documents, and the pen that Admiral Nimitz used are on permanent display at the U.S. Naval Academy Museum in Annapolis, Maryland.

Until called to support United Nations Forces in embattled in Korea in 1950, the *Missouri* trained thousands of naval reserves, midshipmen, and other naval personnel on cruises from New England to the Caribbean and across the Atlantic to English and European waters.

Leaving Norfolk 19 August 1950, the *Missouri* became the first American battleship to reach Korean waters just one day in advance of the Inchon landings on September 15, 1950. As the flagship of Rear Admiral A. E. Smith, she engaged in bombarding Samchok in a diversionary move coordinated with the Inchon landings. In company with the cruiser *Helena* and two destroyers, she helped prepare the way for the Eighth Army offensive. In a bombardment of the Pohang area 17 September 1950, the *Missouri*'s 16-inch shells assisted the South Korean troops in the capture of that town and their advance on Yongdok.

On 7 October, the *Missouri* became the flagship of Vice Adm. Arthur D. Struble, commander of the Seventh Fleet. Her bombardment of the Mitsubishi Iron Works and the airfield at Chongjin on 12 October was a significant factor in the advance of American and other United Nations forces. Her guns did considerable damage to marshaling yards and a strategic railroad bridge in the Tanchon area. Following the entry of the Communist Chinese into the war on the side of North Korean, the *Missouri* moved on to bombard Wonsan and Hungnam. There her powerful guns provided cover for the evacuation of U.S. Marines, other United Nations troops, and South Koreans shortly before Christmas 1950.

In the opening weeks of 1951, the *Missouri* continued coastal bombardment of transportation facilities to disrupt the flow of enemy reinforcements and supplies to central Korea. She joined a heavy bombardment group off Kansong on 29 January 1951 and during the first week of February, gave fire support for the advance of the Tenth U.S. Army on Kangnung. She systematically bombarded transportation facilities and enemy troop concentrations in the vicinity of Tanchon, Songjin, Kojo Wan, Songjin, Chaho, and Wonsan. On 28 March, 1951, the *Missouri* was relieved of duty in the Far East. She arrived in Norfolk on 27 April 1951. On 18 October 1951, she entered the Norfolk Naval Shipyard for an overhaul, which lasted until 30 January 1952.

On 4 August 1952, the *Missouri* was again in the Norfolk Naval Shipyard for overhaul being prepared for her second tour in the Korean Combat Zone. By the end of October, as flagship of the U.S. Seventh Fleet, she provided artillery support for Republic of Korea troops in the Chaho area. Throughout the remaining months of 1952, the *Missouri* was on "Cobra Patrol" along the east coast of Korea, hitting Chongjin, the Tanchon-Songjin area, Chaho, and Wonsan. During the bombardment of the Hamhung and Hungnam areas, the *Missouri* lost three of her men when her spotter helicopter crashed into the sea on 21 December 1952. Early in 1953, the *Missouri* made repeated gun strikes in direct support of troops on land. Her last fighting mission of the Korean War was on 25 March 1953 when she bombarded the Kojo area.

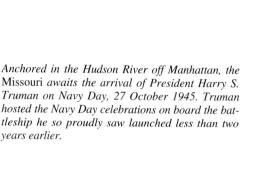
Anchored in the Hudson River off Manhattan, the Missouri *awaits the arrival of President Harry S. Truman on Navy Day, 27 October 1945. Truman hosted the Navy Day celebrations on board the battleship he so proudly saw launched less than two years earlier.*

The *Missouri* was relieved as flagship on 6 April and arrived at Norfolk 4 May 1953. Following a midshipmen training cruise to Brazil, Trinidad, Panama, and Cuba, she went into the Norfolk Naval Shipyard for an overhaul from 20 November 1953 to 2 April 1954. In August 1954, she left Norfolk for the West Coast where she was decommissioned 26 February 1955 and assigned as headquarters ship of the Bremerton Group, U.S. Pacific Reserve Fleet. At Bremerton, as many as 100,000 people a year visited the *Missouri* to see the place on her deck where the Japanese surrendered ending the Second World War.

Interest in activating units of the *Iowa* class began after a 1977 survey of the four ships. They were found structurally sound with at least fifteen years of active service life remaining in each. Their re-activation was seen as a quick improvement to U.S. Naval surface capabilities. Following the *Iowa* and *New Jersey* back into active service, the *Missouri* left her berth at the Bremerton Group on 14 May 1984. She entered the Long Beach Naval Shipyard for reactivation and modernization, which continued into 1985. The *Missouri* was finally ready for duty and in the opening months of 1986, got underway under her own power, and the thunder of her guns was heard for the first time in more than thirty years. Following her recommissioning in San Francisco on 10 May, she scored higher in her gunfire qualifications than any battleship had ever scored.

The *Missouri* got underway on 10 September 1986 for the first circumnavigation of the globe by a battleship since the Great White Fleet in 1907–1909. Back in Long Beach during the first half of 1987, she underwent the last of her reactivation and modernization. On 9 July, she began a year of at-sea exercises and deployment in the Western Pacific, Indian Ocean, and the North Arabian Sea.

On 17 January 1950, standing out to sea on a training cruise, the Missouri *ran hard aground a mile and a half from the Thimble Shoals Light off Old Point Comfort, Virginia. She was finally refloated on 1 February after a massive salvage operation. Some of her bottom plates had been ripped open, but she suffered no serious damage and was soon back in operating condition.*

Left: the battleships Missouri *and* New Jersey *lie moored together at same buoy in Yokosuka on 20 April 1953. The* New Jersey *relieved the* Missouri *on 6 April as flagship of the Seventh Fleet. Almost seven months earlier the* Iowa *and* Missouri *were moored to the same buoy when the latter relieved the* Iowa *as flagship of the Seventh Fleet. The* Missouri *was soon homeward bound and called at Annapolis on 6 June to embark midshipmen for their summer cruise (see photo page 37).*

Below left: the crew and midshipmen celebrate the fourth anniversary of the Japanese surrender during the Naval Academy midshipmen's summer cruise in 1949. They are gathered around the plaque marking the spot where Japan surrendered.

During "Earnest Will" operations in October and November, the *Missouri* provided surface protection for U.S. flagged tankers and their escorts transiting the Strait of Hormuz.

On 24 November, the *Missouri* was relieved and arrived at Long Beach Naval Station on 19 January 1988. Highlights of 1988 included a successful firing of her "first ever" Tomahawk missile on 25 May and participation in multinational Pacific Rim exercises in the Hawaii and Southern California operating areas. In November, the *Missouri* became the first recipient of the USS *Arizona* Memorial Trophy as the battleship achieving the greatest combat readiness score during the eighteen-month competitive cycle.

The year 1989 began with a dry dock period from 25 April to May 24. Back on duty, she took part in a joint U.S.-Japan exercise, which culminated in a fire-power demonstration off Okinawa on 14 October, when the ship fired 263 rounds of 5-inch shells and 45 16-inch projectiles. The *Missouri* ended the year with a visit to Mexico.

Throughout 1990, the *Missouri* was underway training and conducting weapons tests. She again participated in Pacific Rim exercises with more than 55 ships, 200 aircraft, and 50,000 armed forces from the U.S., Japan, Korea, Australia, and Canada. On 21 June, during operations in the Southern California

Right and below: the Missouri *arrived back in her home port, Norfolk, on 27 April 1951, after completing her first Korean tour. Tugs ease the huge battleship into Pier 7 at the main base. Docking operations are being completed as relatives and friends wait to be reunited with their navy men. To starboard of the* Missouri *are the cruisers* Albany *(CA123) and* Macon *(CA132). Forward of the* Albany *and* Macon *is the aft end of the* Hornet's *(CV12) flight deck.*

area, the ship was on target when she launched her first Harpoon cruise missile. Then, at the end of July, the ship's captain received word that she was likely to be inactivated and decommissioned. World events soon changed that when Iraq's President Saddam Hussein invaded Kuwait. Any plans to inactivate the *Missouri* were put on hold.

That fall, the *Missouri*'s crew received training in naval gunfire support, firefighting, basic chemical, biological, and radiological defense, and damage control, among other things. In November, the *Missouri* received five remotely piloted vehicles (RPV) for use as spotters in gunnery and missile targeting. Then, with full international media coverage, she left Long Beach at 1400 on 13 November to join the battleship *Wisconsin* on station in support of Operation Desert Shield in the Persian Gulf.

Christmas was spent at sea, and then, on 3 January 1991, when the *Missouri* steamed into the Persian Gulf, the tempo of operations increased significantly. No sooner had she transited the Strait of Hormuz, than the ship was on the scene to aid a merchant ship on fire in the southern Gulf. Her firefighting team and equipment quickly put out the fire.

As the battleship made her way through mine-laced waters, her explosive ordnance disposal team destroyed their first mine on 9 January 1991. Mine spotting and destroying operations continued until the *Missouri* reached Manama, Bahrain on 15 January there to await the 0800 deadline on 16 January, for Iraq's withdrawal from Kuwait. Four hours after the deadline, the *Missouri* was underway, and at 0140 on 17 January 1991, she fired her first Tomahawk missile in bat-

Above: the Missouri *fires a Tomahawk missile on the morning of 17 January 1991, the first day of the Allied offensive against Iraq in Operation Desert Storm. Note the sand bags on deck to protect the crew in case of an attack by fast Iraqi patrol boats. Above right: An Iraqi mine floats near the* Missouri *prior to being detonated by an Explosive Ordnance Disposal (EOD) team. Floating mines were a constant danger in the Persian Gulf during Operation Desert Shield and Storm, and a few that were not located are still navigational hazzards*

tle. During the first three days of Desert Storm, she fired twenty-five Tomahawk missiles and three more over the next two days. On Sunday night, 3 February, the *Missouri* fired on Iraqi positions in occupied Kuwait in support of U.S. Marines ashore, which was the first time since the Korean War that the *Missouri*'s 16-inch guns were fired in a hostile action. It also marked the first wartime use of an RPV for gun fire spotting. The following day, the battleship's guns continued to pound Iraqi positions and then, she moved north, once more in mine-filled waters. Over the following days, she provided fire support against artillery batteries, radar control and logistics sites, suspected headquarters and command and control bunkers, infantry battalions, a mechanized unit, and an artillery battery. Continuing north, the ship evaded several minefields and destroyed her tenth mine while deployed for Desert Storm. The USS *Tripoli* and USS *Princeton* were not as lucky. Both struck mines, and damage suffered by the Tripoli led to the brief transfer of the Task Group Commander's flag to the "Mighty Mo." In addition to mines, the crew of the *Missouri* had to deal with the threat of an Iraqi chemical weapons attack. They operated regularly at "mission-oriented protective posture," or MOPP, levels, wearing the cumbersome anti-chemical suits and gas masks.

On Saturday evening, 23 February, the *Missouri* opened fire on Faylaka Island, and then before sunrise, trained her guns on Iraqi targets in Kuwait in support of the ground offensive by U.S. and coalition forces. She continued her barrage through Monday when between 0300 and 0500, she fired more than 125 tons of ordnance on four Iraqi targets. The Iraqis responded with a Silkworm missile,

The Missouri *fires a salvo from her forward turrets on 6 February 1991 during night shore bombardment of the northern Kuwaiti coast. The action is seen from the mine watch position at the bow. The* Missouri *and her sister the* Wisconsin *were used for numerous softening-up strikes against the Kuwaiti coast in case an amphibious landing became necessary.*

which was shot down with Sea Dart anti-missile missiles by HMS *Gloucester*, which was operating in company with the *Missouri*. By Tuesday morning, when the *Missouri* was relieved, she had fired 611 rounds of 16-inch shells, or more than 1,100,000 pounds of ordnance, in sixty hours of shore bombardment. On 21 March, the battleship left the Persian Gulf for Long Beach.

The year ended with a trip to Pearl Harbor for the 7 December observances, where the *Missouri* served as the viewing platform for the ceremonies at the *Arizona* Memorial. President George Bush was aboard for "Operation Remembrance," the first President on her decks since President Harry Truman embarked in September 1947.

On 16 December, the *Missouri* was at Seal Beach to off-load ammunition and missiles in preparation for decommissioning. She was underway under her own power for the last time at 1637 on 20 December 1991, on her way to the Long Beach Naval Station. She spent Christmas and New Year's moored at pier six, awaiting decommissioning preparations to begin on 6 January 1992.

The Mighty Mo was decommissioned for the second time on 31 March 1992 after which she was towed to Bremerton, Washington. On 5 January 1995, she and the three other *Iowa*s were removed from the navy's lists, which was the first step toward her new career as a memorial museum. Under the auspices of the Honolulu-based USS *Missouri* Memorial Association, which is responsible for preserving her as a historic ship memorial, she was moved to Ford Island to take her place next to the *Arizona* Memorial at Pearl Harbor in 1998. And though the *Missouri*'s active duty life has ended, her mission to carry on the heritage of the U.S. Navy's last battleships, to tell the story of the events of which they were a part, and to honor the men who served on them continues in the twenty-first century.

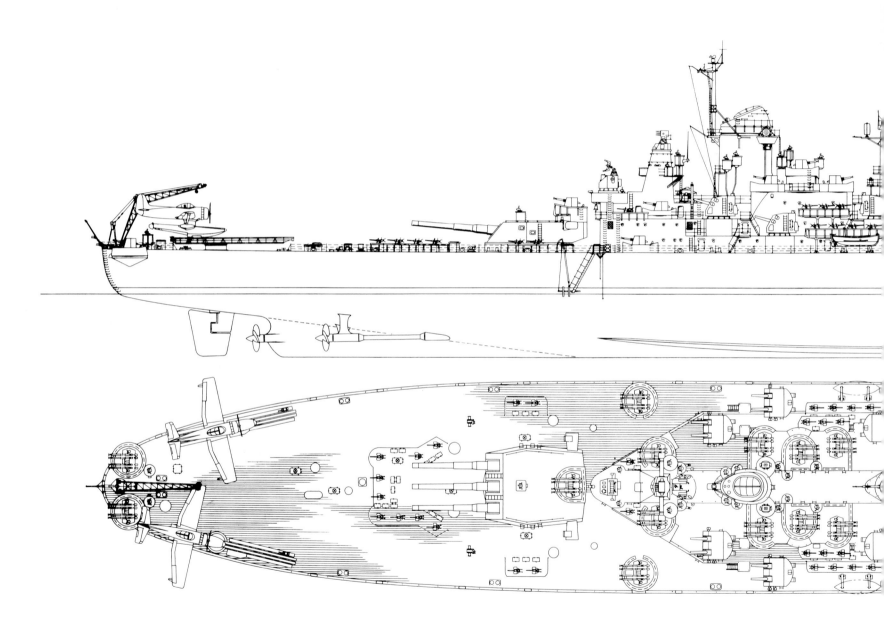

Drawings by Robert F. Sumrall

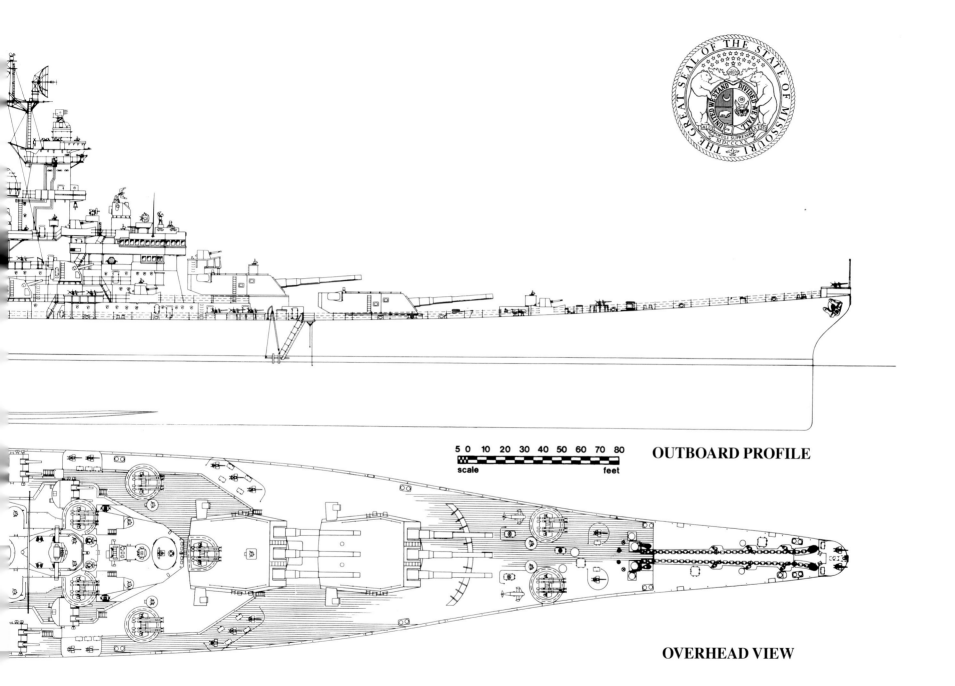

OUTBOARD PROFILE

scale   feet

OVERHEAD VIEW

GENERAL DATA

HULL

Name: United States Ship MISSOURI
Hull Number: BB 63
Builder: New York Navy Yard
Laid Down: 6 January 1941
Launched: 29 January 1944
Commissioned: 11 June 1944

Displacement:
45,000 tons Standard (1945)
57,540 tons Full Load (1945)
900 tons Trial Load (19 45)

Dimensions:
887´ 3˝ Length Overall
860´ Waterline Length
108´ 2˝ Maximum Beam
4´ Frame Spacing - 216 Frames

MACHINERY

Boilers:
Eight B&W three-drum, double-furnace, express-type
Pressure: 565 psi
Temperature: 850º F

Turbines: Four sets General Electric geared turbines

Reduction:
Four sets General Electric double-reduction
Shaft HP: 212,000
Shaft RPM: 202

Speed: 33 knots

Generators:
Eight ship's-service, 450-volt, 3-phase, AC (1,250 KW)
Two emergency diesel (250 KW)

Shafts: Four

Propellers:
Two five-bladed, 17´ 0˝ inboard
Two four-bladed, 18´ 3˝ outboard

Rudders:
Two semi-balanced streamlined-type; projected area, 340 sq. ft. each

Draft/Loading: 37´ 9˝ @ 57,540 tons
154 tons per inch immersion
Decommissioned: 26 February 1955
Recommissioned: 10 May 1986
Decommissioned: 31 March 1992

Complement:
Officer	189 (1945), 151 (1949), 65 (1986)
Enlisted	2,789 (1945), 2,255 (1949), 1445 (1986)

Fuel Oil: 8,841 tons
Diesel Oil: 182 tons
Gasoline: 8,588 gallons

ARMOR PROTECTION

Amidships:	Main Belt	12.1˝ on 0.875 STS inclined 19 degrees
	Lower Belt	12.1˝ tapered to 1.625˝ on 0.875 STS inclined 19 degrees
	Main Deck	1.50˝
	Second Deck	4.75˝ + 1.25˝
	Splinter Deck	0.625˝
	Third Deck	0.625˝
Turret:	Face Plates	17.0˝ + 2.7˝
	Sides	9.5˝
	Back Plates	12.0˝
	Roof	7.25˝
Secondary:	Mounts	2.5˝
	Handling Rooms	2.5˝
Barbette:	Top to 2nd Deck	17.3˝ - 11.6˝
	2nd to 3rd Deck	3˝
	Below 3rd Deck	1.5˝
Conning Tower:	Sides	17.5˝
	Roof	7.25˝
	Deck	4˝
	Tube	16˝

Acknowledgments

This is a completely rewritten version of Pictorial Histories Warship's Data 2, which I wrote in 1986. The original publication was written before the *Missouri* was recommissioned in 1986, and a second part was planned for the history of the ship from that date on. It seemed reasonable to put all of the material in one volume and keep its original publication number in the series. A considerable amount of material and photographs has been added to bring this new book up to date, including the ship's recent arrival and berthing in Pearl Harbor as a memorial. All of the line drawings are taken from my originals. The renderings are by Paul Bender and John R. Barrett who have worked with me on a number of publications of this type in the past.

I would like to thank a number of individuals at the Naval Historical Center for their continued help and assistance. They are: Charles Haberlein, Edwin Finney, John Reilly, Jr., Mark Wortheimer, Cal Cavalconte, and Kathleen Lloyd. Don Montgomery at the Naval Imaging Command was invaluable with photo research, and Ken Johnson was a great help in finding records and data at the National Archives II at College Park, Md. Finally, my assistant, Ann Jensen, deserves special recognition for the many hours spent in organizing and editing the manuscript.

Robert F. Sumrall

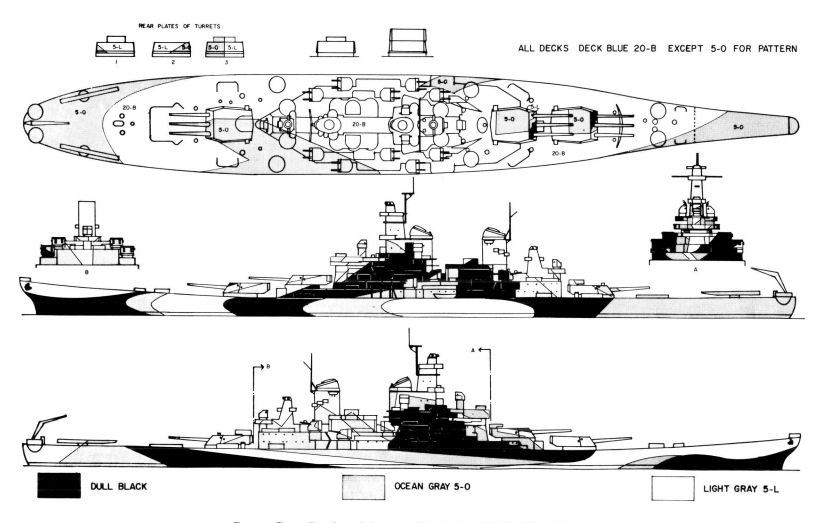

REAR PLATES OF TURRETS

ALL DECKS DECK BLUE 20-B EXCEPT 5-O FOR PATTERN

DULL BLACK

OCEAN GRAY 5-O

LIGHT GRAY 5-L

Camouflage Design: Measure 32, Design 22 D, May 1944

CAMOUFLAGE

During her shakedown period in 1944, the *Missouri* was painted in camouflage Measure 32, Design 22 D. This dazzle, or disruptive, pattern was the best all-around antiaircraft measure applicable to any type of vessel. Although highly visible to submarines, the pattern distorted the silhouette making an approach for torpedo attack difficult.

In January 1945, during an availability at Long Beach on her way to the

Far East, the *Missouri* was painted in Measure 22 camouflage. According to this pattern, all vertical surfaces were painted in HAZE GRAY (5-H) with a NAVY BLUE (5-N) band on the hull running parallel to the waterline from the lowest point of sheer down. She finished the war in this pattern.

Early in 1946, the *Missouri* was painted in standard HAZE GRAY on all vertical surfaces and DECK BLUE on all horizontal surfaces.

ARMAMENT SUMMARY FOR USS MISSOURI (BB-63)

WEAPON	June 1944	April 1945	Sept. 1945	June 1946	Jan. 1947	Oct. 1947	April 1951	April 1952	May 1986
16-inch/50 cal. triple:	9	9	9	9	9	9	9	9	9
5-inch/38 cal. twin:	20	20	20	20	20	20	20	20	12
40 mm quad:	20	20	20	20	20	20	10	20	
20 mm single:	49	49	43	26	22				
20 mm twin		8	8	8	8	16	32		
20 mm CIWS									4
RGM-84 Harpoon									16
BGM-109 Tomahawk									32

NOTES: 1. This tabulation was taken from the Armament Summaries of the Bureau of Naval Ordnance, 1943 through 1955 and the current Ship's Allowance List.
2. Actual intallation of twin 20 mms in 1945 is uncertain.
3. The ultimate approved anti-aircraft battery from the April 1955 Summary was 16, 3-inch/50 caliber twin mounts.

REPRESENTATIVE MISSILE ROUNDS

Weapon/Desig.	Item	Warhead Wt (lb.)	Type	MK	Speed (Mach.) Cruise	Attack	Propellant Cruise	Boost	Range Mode	NM	Guidance
BGM-109	1	1,000	HE		0.50	0.75	Liquid	Solid	TSAM	470	Active Radar
Tomahawk	2	980	HE		0.50	0.75	Liquid	Solid	TLAM-C	675	TERCOM
	3	293	HE-N		0.50	0.75	Liquid	Solid	TLAM-N	1,500	TERCOM
RGM-84	4	510	HE		0.82	0.87	Liquid	Solid	RBL	64	Active Radar
Harpoon	5	510	HE		0.82	0.87	Liquid	Solid	BOL	85	Active Radar

NOTES: 1. The above information has been compiled from unclassified and published sources.

REPRESENTATIVE SERVICE ROUNDS

Gun/Caliber	Item	Projectiles Wt (lb.)	Type	MK	Velocity (f/s)[2]	Powder	Propellant Wt. (lb.)	Charge	Sections	Assembly	Maximum Range El.	Yards[3]
16"/50	[1]1	2,240	A.P.	5	2,700	SPD	640	Full	6	Stacked	45°	47,000
MK7	2	2,700	A.P.	8	2,500	SPD	660	Full	6	Stacked		42,500
RPM:2	3	2,700	A.P.	8	1,800	SPD/N	420	Target	6	Stacked		24,000
	4	2,700	A.P.	8	1,800	SPD/N/CG	305	Reduced	6	Dumped		
	5	1,900	H.C.	13	2,690	SPD	660	Full	6	Stacked	45°	41,600
	6	1,900	H.C.	13	2,075	SPD/N/CG	305	Reduced	6	Dumped		27,379
	7	1,900	H.C.	13	1,900	SPD	325	Reduced	6	Dumped		
	8	1,900	H.E.	14	2,690	SPD	660	Full	6	Stacked		
	9	1,900	HE/CVT	143	2,690	SPD	660	Full	6	Stacked		
	10	1,880	ICM	144	2,690	SPD	660	Full	6	Stacked		
	11	1,900	HE/ET	145	2,690	SPD	660	Full	6	Stacked		
	12	1,900	ICM	146	2,690	SPD	660	Full	6	Stacked		

NOTES: 1. The gun was originally designed to use the 2,240 lb. A.P. projectile. The 2,700 lb. projectile was adopted in 1939.
2. Projectiles MK 143, 144, 145, & 146 use a modified MK 13 body.
3. Altered ballistics depending on when/where munitions are dispensed. Impact of projectile body approx. 2,000 yards down range from point where munitions are dispensed.

REPRESENTATIVE SERVICE ROUNDS

Gun/Caliber	Item	Wt (lb.)	Type	MK	Velocity (f/s)	Powder	Wt. (lb.)	Charge	El.	Yards	El.	Feet
			Projectiles				Propellant		Maximum Range		Maximum Altitude	
5"/38(1)	1	53.3	H.C.	35	2,600	(2)	15.5-17(2)	Full	45°	18,200	85°	37,200
MK12	2	55.1	A.A.C.	35	2,600	(2)	15.5-17(2)	Full	45°	18,200	85°	37,200
RPM:15	3	54.3	ILLUM	50	2,600	(2)	15.5-17(2)	Full	45°	(3)	(3)	(3)
	4	54.5	WP	50	2,600	(2)	15.5-17(2)	Full	45°	18,200	(3)	(3)
40mm(4)	5	1.96	A.P.	81	2,890	SPDN	300 gms.	Full	42°	11,000	90°	22,800
(1.57°/60)	6	1.985	A.A.C.	1/2	2,890	SPDN	300 gms.	Full	42°	11,000	90°	22,800
RPM:160												
20mm(5)	7	0.269	A.P.-T.	9	2,740	SPDN	27.7 gms.	Full	35°	4,800	90°	10,000
(0.8/70)	8	0.271	H.E.	3	2,740	SPDN	27.7 gms.	Full	35°	4,800	90°	10,000
MK 4	9	0.274	H.E./T.	7	2,740	SPDN	27.7 gm.	Full	35°	4,800	90°	10,000
RPM: 450												
20mm(6)	10	0.156	A.P.	149	3,700	WS-19781/ 650 gns.		Full	45°	11,750		
CIWS Phalanx six-barrel RPM: 3,000												

NOTES: 1. There were and are a large number of 5"/38 projectiles available for all purposes. The rounds represented are typical of WII and current ammunition being used.
2. The types of powder in use for all service rounds listed is SPD, SPDN, and SPDF.
3. Altered ballistics depending on when/where illumination or smoke is desired.
4. A.P. penetrates 1.7" max. @1,000 yds. Tracer burns out @ 5,000 yds. horizontal, 15,000 ft. vertical.
5. Tracer burns out @ 3,000 yds.
6. Sabot round with sub-caliber heavy metal penetrator of depleted uranium. No other data available.

ARMOR PENETRATION
2,700 lb. MK 8 Projectile @ 2,425 f/s IV(1)

Armor Class	Range/yards	Angle of Fall°	Striking Velocity f/s	Penetration in inches
Class "A"	14,600	9.86°	1,682	22"
	21,400	17.52°	1,661	18"
Vertical	29,500	29.08°	1,530	14"
	39,200	48.74°	1,583	10"
Class "B"	15,250	10.58°	1,839	3"
	23,700	20.59°	1,610	5"
Horizontal	32,700	34.92°	1,515	8"
	39,250	48.90°	1,583	12"

NOTES: 1. Data from ORD 653(c) using initial velocity of a gun with a liner worn to the average life of the liner.

REINFORCED CONCRETE PENETRATION
Slab Concrete (5,000 psi)

Projectile Type	Range/ yards	Angle of Fall°	Striking Velocity f/s	Thickness in ft. Obliquity 0°	30°
2,700 lb. A.P. MK8	10,000	6°	2,074	27.5´	20.5´
	20,000	15°	1,748		
@	30,000	28°	1,567	18.5´	14.0´
2,500 f/sIV(1)	42,345	53°	1,686	20.0´	15.0´
1,900 lb.	10,000	5°	2,083	16.5´	13.0´
H.C. MK13	20,000	16°	1,606	12.5´	9.5´
@	30,000	32°	1,391	10.5´	8.0´
2,690 f/sIV(1)	41,622	57°	1,552	12.0´	9.5´

NOTES: 1. Data from O.P. 1172 using initial velocity of a gun with a new liner.

The Missouri *visits pearl Harbor in observance of the 50th anniversary of the Japanese attack. She is shown here on 7 December 1991 in dress ship with tourists aboard.*

The water is illuminated as the Missouri *fires a full nine-gun broadside during target practice shortly after her recommissioning in 1986. The weight of the nine armor piercing projectiles was 24,300 pounds.*

The Missouri *arrives at Pearl Harbor on 22 June 1998 to begin her final deployment as a museum ship. The battleship looms over a gathering of fans as she makes her way to her new home at mooring FOX 5 on Ford Island where the battleships* Maryland *(BB-46) and* Oklahoma *(BB-37) were moored at the time of the Japanese attack on Pearl Harbor.*

For further information about the USS *Missouri* contact:
USS *Missouri* Memorial Association, Inc.
P.O. Box 6339
Honolulu, Hawaii 96818
http://www.ussmissouri.com